BUM-BELIEVABLE!

A mind-bending collection of facts

Ian Locke

THE BUMper BOOK OF FACTs

MACMILLAN CHILDREN'S BOOKS

st books 1998 and 1999
s Books

millan Children's Books
shers Limited
on N1 9RR
Basingstoke and Oxford
Associated companies throughout the world
www.panmacmillan.com

ISBN 978-1-4472-2610-9

Contents

Crazy Creatures

The giant squid is one of the longest creatures on earth – it can grow up to 15 metres or 45 foot. It also has the largest eyes of any living animal; they are up to 38 cm across.

A female elephant will always adopt a baby elephant which has lost its mother.

Evelyn Françon of France found his cat Graffiti messy and noisy and gave him away to friends 100 miles away when he moved to a new job in 1995. A few months later his friends told him that Graffiti had run away. In January 1997 Evelyn heard a scratching and screeching at his front door. It was Graffiti! The cat had spent two years making the journey through the foothills of the French Alps to his old owner's new home in Isère. Evelyn said, 'I shall have to keep him now.'

A dog's sense of smell can be amazing. A Doberman once tracked a sheep thief for 100 miles by scent alone across the Great Karoo plain in South Africa.

There are 30 species of slug in Britain.

The rattlesnake or viper has special cells between its nostril and its eye. These are sensitive to infrared radiant heat and can locate people in the dark by the heat they give off.

 The male emperor penguin looks after the egg of its young for between 105 and 115 days in a temperature of about -16°C. During this time it has nothing to eat and only survives by huddling together with other males on ice floes.

 48 rats were on the space shuttle Columbia in 1993.

The fastest growing creature on Earth is the blue whale. From the time it begins growing to full growth it increases up to 30,000 million times in size.

The giant megamouth shark was discovered by the US Navy in 1976.

Any type of rabbit can be a pet. Among the names of types of rabbits are Rex, British Giant, Dwarf Lop and Netherland Dwarf. A British Giant rabbit can grow to twice the size of a fully grown cat and weigh up to 12 kg.

The only poisonous bird is the orange and black songbird, the hooded Pitohui, discovered by accident in New Guinea in 1992.

 Charles Cruft, who started the famous Cruft's dog shows in London, never owned a dog and never went to his shows. He had a pet cat.

The average caterpillar has 16 legs.

The first cat working for the Post Office, to catch mice, arrived in London in 1868. The cats which were used by the Post Office in Britain were paid 'a shilling [5p] a week and all the mice you can catch'. By 1983 the pay of cats was £2 a week.

 Some dogs can become very attached to their masters. Among the strangest stories of such closeness is that of Susie, a fox terrier owned by Lord Carnarvon. Lord Carnarvon, who put up the money for the finding of the tomb of Tutankhamun in Egypt, was dying in Cairo, the capital of Egypt. He had blood poisoning from an infected mosquito bite. Back in England, at his stately home of Highclere, Susie went downstairs and fell dead in the hall. It was exactly the same time that her master died. Why or how this happened no one can explain.

The blue whale can grow up to over 30 metres long and weigh over 100 tonnes. It is the longest and heaviest animal ever known to have lived. The female is larger than the male. They can eat up to about 1,000 kg of the plankton krill at one time. When born, the baby blue whale, called a calf, is about 7 metres long.

The average woodpecker pecks 20 times a second.

The biggest bird known to have lived in recent times is the Madagascan elephant bird which died out 300 years ago, in about 1660. Its egg was 30 cm large and could hold 7 litres. It was also known as the 'Roc bird', was about 3 metres high and weighed nearly 500 kg. The name of the bird was used in the *Tales of Sinbad*.

A bite from a black mamba snake, which can grow up to 4 metres long, nearly always kills a person. The snake lives in south and central Africa. When the snake bites, a person will feel dizzy, then find it difficult to breathe, then the heart beats erratically until the person dies.

A monkey called Johnny learned to drive a tractor on a sheep farm near Melbourne, Australia. Johnny began just as a pet of the farm's owner, but soon learned to open and shut gates after copying his master. When he learned to drive the tractor he somehow knew that it had to be started in neutral. Johnny drove the tractor in a straight line or along a path on signals and calls from his owner. At lunchtime the monkey had his own lunchbag, putting the litter back in the bag after he'd finished.

The world's most travelled cat is probably a three-year-old tabby called Tabitha, owned by American actress Carol Timmel. In 1995 Tabitha escaped from her carrier when she was in a jumbo jet flying across America. After a search she could not be found. Over the next 12 days the jumbo continued to fly back and forth across America. During this time Tabitha's owner decided that the airline, Tower Air, had not made a proper search for her pet. So, when the jumbo landed, a second search for Tabitha was made. She was eventually found hiding behind a passenger compartment. Apart from being dirty, she was fine. No one was admitting what she might have eaten during her 12 days' journey. The total number of miles she flew while wandering the plane was over 30,000!

The tarantula spider is said to be dangerous, but its bite is really harmless; at worst it causes only a little swelling and some pain.

A tortoise can live for up to 200 years; by contrast the usual lifespan of a hamster is only four years. A tortoise which died in 1966 was 188 years old. It was presented to the King of Tonga in 1773 by Captain Cook.

The sea otter never gets its skin wet when it goes in the sea. It has two coats of fur, which keep its skin perfectly dry.

Emperor Napoleon of France was terrified by cats.

The first guide dogs were used in Germany in a home for blind people, in 1916. The first ever guide dog was called Excelsior. He was trained by a Doctor Gorlitz to lead a blind man across the lawn. After this worked, guide dogs were used all over Germany, then all over the world.

 Judy, an English dog, was a hero during the Second World War. She was born in the city of Shanghai in China. She was looked after by men of the British Royal Navy aboard a gunboat. One day the gunboat was torpedoed by the Japanese Navy. Judy and some of the men were taken prisoner. She spent two years in a Japanese prison camp on the island of Sumatra. Her owners were used as slaves by the Japanese to build a railway. During the time she was a prisoner Judy attacked the Japanese guards and helped prisoners who were about to be beaten. In 1945 she and her fellow prisoners were rescued and released.

A mother cat, Scarlett, became a heroine in Brooklyn, New York, in April 1996. A fire broke out in an abandoned building. Several floors up, the stray Scarlett began to rescue all her five kittens, one by one. In and out she went. She carried each of them down in her mouth, made sure they were all right and went back into the fire. Each time her red fur got more burned and her eyes were seared by the heat. Finally she got the last of her kittens out. She stood guard over them until they were all rescued by firemen. Scarlett and her kittens all recovered. Hundreds of people heard the story and wanted to look after Scarlett and the kittens.

A fly's taste buds are in its feet.

When on land, otters use their tail as a third leg to stand up, strut across the ground or peer over objects in their path. When underwater, small flaps on their ears close up so they do not get water in them.

An ostrich's intestines are up to 15 metres long.

Bats can get too hot and get heat-stroke. Thousands of bats were affected by the heat in Fort Worth, Texas, USA, in 1989. They fell out of the sky on to buildings and into the busy streets.

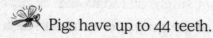 A cow's sweat glands are in its nose. Cow's noses are like human fingerprints – they can be used to identify the cow.

 The okapi is one of the world's strangest animals. It has eyes that can look both ways at the same time, a see-through tongue which is up to 35 cm long, and four stomachs. It has the legs of a zebra, the body of an antelope, the walk of a giraffe, the speed of an ostrich and the courage of a tiger. They spend almost all their lives on their own.

 Pigs have up to 44 teeth.

The turkey was given its name by the British. The French called this American bird the Indian bird. In Turkey they are called 'American birds'.

The first turtle was brought to London in 1752 by Admiral Anson. Turtles and tortoises cannot move their ribs, so they breathe by pushing air through their necks. Turtles' necks have an extra water supply.

In the nineteenth century a clergyman in England found a brown rat in his house. The rat soon became a pet and quite tame. One night the man was woken up by the rat biting his cheek. Looking around he found to his alarm that the curtains on his four-poster bed were on fire. The man quickly made his way out of the house, which was burned to the ground. Unfortunately he was never to see his heroic pet again.

Hannibal, the general who led the army of the city of Carthage against the Romans almost two thousand years ago, became famous for crossing the Alps. In his army he had 90,000 soldiers on foot, 12,000 cavalry and 37 elephants. The poor elephants were not suited to the cold and length of this journey into Italy. Only one of them is supposed to have survived.

The great horned owl is the only animal that will eat skunk.

The ancient Egyptian army was once defeated by cats! The King of Persia came up with a plan. He sent soldiers with cats in their arms at the head of his army. The Egyptians, who treated cats as gods and did not dare harm them, surrendered.

In Oregon, in the United States, a kitten became friends with a 250 kg grizzly bear at a wildlife park. When the starving kitten first arrived, in 1995, the grizzly took out a piece of chicken from its food bucket and gave it to the hungry kitten.

Shrews have two sorts of sounds – they twitter and scream. They only scream when they meet another shrew.

Manx cats of the Isle of Man have no tails.

Packs of wolves travel up to 50 miles from their lairs in their search for food. When they move, they always try and keep to a straight line, moving at a trot.

African elephants stay on their feet for 30 or 40 years.

The dolphin can swim at up to 24 miles an hour.

The European oyster starts its life as a male, then changes into a female.

The ancient Egyptians shaved off their eyebrows to mourn the death of their cats.

 Tuna fish swim at an average speed of 9 miles an hour all the time; they never stop moving.

Ants seem to have monthly holidays when they do nothing.

Snakes cannot cry. They do not have eyelids. Instead their eyes are protected by a clear skin.

Only half the world's spiders spin webs; the rest of them hunt for their food. The largest web is spun by the tropical golden-orb web spider. Its web can be up to 1.5 m across and held up by lines up to 6 m long. The smallest web is made by the midget spider, less than 12 mm across. The web of a garden spider can have up to 30 m of strong silk; this silk can be stretched six times its length without breaking then return to normal size. It is stronger than steel.

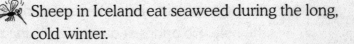 Earthworms have five hearts.

Sheep in Iceland eat seaweed during the long, cold winter.

Seals have been known to swim for as long as 8 months and as far as 6,000 miles without touching land.

 The kangaroo cannot jump if its tail is lifted off the ground.

11

In Africa, elephants discovered a sort of penicillin before people. Sick elephants were seen using a type of slimy mould for wounds and drank it to make them better. Local native people saw this and began using the slime for their own cuts and sores.

 Jellyfish sometimes evaporate.

 Dolphins have bigger brains than humans.

Rabbits can talk to each other by thumping their feet.

The hornbill bird has very odd behaviour when nesting. The female bird, which has a large clumsy beak, looks for a hollow in a tree where she can lay her eggs. As soon as the eggs are laid, the male starts filling up the hole. He brings in damp clay, filling the hole until there is only a small opening for the female's beak. The clay dries solid and the female is walled in until the eggs hatch. The male feeds her through the gap which is left. When the chicks are born, both parents break down the hard wall.

Swordfish can reach speeds of 60 miles an hour.

Baboons cannot throw overarm.

An electric eel will short-circuit if it is put in salt, rather than fresh, water.

A duck will often swim while sleeping.

All polar bears are left-handed. Polar bear mothers usually have twins. They are the size of rats when born and are blind for a month.

A newborn panda is smaller than a mouse.

Deadly Deep

 The first mystery of the area which became known as the Bermuda Triangle happened in 1902, when the German cargo ship *Freya* was found abandoned and crewless.

 At least 21 species of shark live in British waters, including the basking shark, the world's second largest fish, which can grow to a length of 15 metres.

 Seals have been known to swim great distances. In April 1998 a bearded seal was found exhausted and hungry on the beach at Mablethorpe, Lincolnshire. After it had been rescued and named Whiskers, it was discovered that it had swum all the way from Greenland. The last time a bearded seal had been seen in Britain was in 1892, on the Norfolk coast.

 The US diving manual lists all sorts of sea creatures as dangerous. One of the strangest of these is the giant clam, which, we are told, can trap people's arms and legs, holding them until they drown. There is, however, no record of anyone drowning after being trapped by a clam.

There are two types of whale: toothed whales and whalebone whales. Whalebone is an elastic horny substance which grows in a series of thin strips in the upper jaw of some whales instead of teeth. It is often used to stiffen parts of dresses.

Along a shark's body there is a series of sensory organs which detect movement in the water. If a person splashes or thrashes in the water, the shark often assumes it is a crippled or wounded body. The best protection from attack is to move slowly in the water and stay in the same position.

The ocean can be up to seven miles (11 km) deep. It is easier to get information from the surface of the moon than from the depths of the ocean.

If the water in the sea were to evaporate it has been calculated that the layer of salt left behind would be seven metres thick.

Though dolphins are intelligent, the smaller-toothed whale is rated the brightest sea creature.

The fastest fish in the world is the sailfish. It can reach a speed of 110 kph or 60 mph.

The blue whale can survive on its own blubber without eating for six months.

 The lowest form of life, algae, appeared in the sea about 1,200 million years ago.

There is a stretch of water off Japan which is known as the Devil or Ghost Sea because many ships and aircraft have disappeared there. It is Japan's Bermuda Triangle. The area is known for its sudden tidal waves and there have been reports of luminous or glowing white water and the sudden appearance of holes or hills in the sea.

 Cod liver oil was used as a medicine as long ago as 1770. It wasn't until 1921 that it was proved to help cure rickets, the disease that makes bones thin, soft and fragile because of lack of vitamin D.

 Sharks can detect blood from a quarter of a mile away. They have two scent detectors on either side of their snout and can follow a scent trail from both sides, thereby homing in on prey.

During the voyage of the steamship *Valhalla* in 1905, two scientists from London Zoo, Edmund Meade-Waldo and Michael Nicholl, reported seeing a deep-sea monster off Brazil. They claimed it was about two metres long and about as thick as a human body. The monster soon disappeared beneath the waves. It was seen again about 14 hours later. The two men said it looked like a submarine just under the surface of the sea. What the creature actually was remains a mystery.

 The first serious voyage to study the deep ocean was made by the British ship *Challenger* in 1872. It investigated the deep sea and found thousands of creatures new to science.

As the flatfish grows into an adult, it changes from swimming vertically to swimming horizontally. Its eyes change position, moving across the forehead so that both eyes are on the left.

Comb-jellies, which make their own light, look like swimming lanterns in the deep. They live at a depth of up to 3,000 metres.

 Fish and fishy creatures don't always live in the sea. Among the more unusual items found in the 212,500 miles of sewers in Britain in 1997 were sea trout, salmon and a salamander. The stranger items included a stuffed gorilla, a set of jail keys and a working organ!

Each year the water level in the northern oceans drops. The missing water does not turn up in the southern oceans. What happens to it remains a mystery.

The starfish has an eye on the end of each of its arms.

The giant squid has eyes that measure over 30 centimetres in diameter.

The human being is not built for diving in deep water. The pressure underwater forces the body joints to grind together.

On the afternoon of 5 December 1945, five US planes had completed a US navy training exercise off a group of small islands near Bermuda. They began their return to their base at Fort Lauderdale, Florida, as a storm began to blow in. They never arrived. No trace of them could be found in the search that followed. The leading pilot, Lieutenant Charles Taylor, last reported that his compasses had failed. Nothing more was heard. The disappearance of Flight 19 was featured in Steven Spielberg's *Close Encounters of the Third Kind*, in which the pilots are abducted by aliens.

Seven types of sharks have been known to attack people:

1. The great white shark
2. The oceanic white-tip shark
3. The tiger shark
4. The mako shark
5. The bull shark
6. The hammerhead shark
7. The cookiecutter shark

 The common dolphin has been seen surfing on the wake of ships, reaching speeds of over 39 kph or 24 mph!

Several 'ghost ships' appear to exist. During July 1975, Dr Jim Thorne, an American aboard the yacht *New Freedom*, heard a crack of thunder and saw flashes of lightning. The storm was so impressive he took some photographs. When the film was developed he got a surprise. On the edge of the pictures there was an image of an old-fashioned, square-rigged sailing ship! He was positive there were no ships close to him during the brief storm.

 The oddest-looking shark is the goblin shark. Its face looks very wrinkled and ancient, and it has a long, rounded horn on its head, above an ugly blunt snout.

The first hatchling of a sand-tiger shark will eat all its other potential brothers and sisters (as eggs) before they are born!

 Most baby seals are born with a soft woolly coat of fur called lanugo. They lose it before they first go in the water.

 David Bushnell pioneered the use of the submarine in warfare. His sub went into action on 6 September 1776 in New York Harbor. It was supposed to bore holes in British ships, put charges in the holes and blow them up. Since the main British ships had copper bottoms to protect them, it wasn't even possible to make the holes.

 The humpback whale is so large it gets covered in barnacles. They have a clever way of getting rid of the little creatures. They go to a warm freshwater river where the barnacles cannot survive so drop off. Having noticed this, sailors used to put their ships into fresh water to remove the barnacles that encrusted the hulls.

 Ice fish are some of the weirdest around. They live in the cold of the Antarctic and have no red blood. They survive on very little oxygen and their hearts are three times the size of red-blooded fish.

In June 1991, the treasure-hunting ship *Deep Sea*, sailing off the coast of Miami, Florida, made a weird find – five World War II bombers, neatly lined up together on the sea floor. The area was an old US bombing range and aircraft were often ditched in a line during the years 1943–5.

 Joshua Slocum, an American, was the first man to sail alone around the world. He ended his three-year journey on 3 July 1898. Curiously, he never learned to swim.

 Turtles have no teeth.

The ship of the English pirate Samuel Bellamy, the *Whydah*, loaded with 180 bags of treasure, sank in a storm off Cape Cod, Massachusetts, in 1717. Only two on board survived, including Welsh carpenter Thomas Davis who told the tale of the ship and its treasure. In July 1984, treasure hunter Barry Clifford found the wreck of the *Whydah* on the seabed. The recovery of the treasure continued until 1988. By the time Barry Clifford and his team had finished they had found a haul of treasure and items from the wreck that were valued at as much as $400 million – £275 million!

During World War II a number of killer whales were stranded around Britain. It is thought this was because of anti-submarine activities which disorientated them.

 During the summer the average temperature of the Red Sea (between Africa and Arabia) is 30°C – almost as warm as the average bath!

 The world's most poisonous snake is found in the sea! It was named after the explorer Sir Edward Belcher in 1849 and its poison is a hundred times more deadly than that of the most venomous snake on land, the western taipan of Australia.

 The 30-centimetre leafy seadragon, a relative of the sea horse, looks like a piece of seaweed.

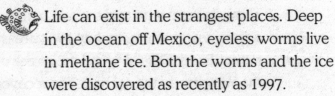 Life can exist in the strangest places. Deep in the ocean off Mexico, eyeless worms live in methane ice. Both the worms and the ice were discovered as recently as 1997.

 The first underwater photos were taken by Louis Boutan of France in a bay off the French coast in 1893.

On 13 January 1852, the crew aboard the whaler *Monongahela* set out from New Bedford, Massachusetts, under the command of Captain Amos Seabury. Not far from Panama, they sighted another US whaler, the *Rebecca Sims*, and soon afterwards the lookout saw a strange shape in the water. Three boats were sent from the *Monongahela*. A huge head on a long neck emerged from the sea – it was twice as big as a whale.

After one boat was wrecked by the creature, the beast was harpooned. A towline was attached to it and the two whalers began hauling it in. Before long the monster died and the whole body floated to the surface. It was 100 metres long with a circumference of about 15 metres. The experienced sailors later described it as similar to a huge alligator. There was no chance of bringing the whole body on board, so the head alone was kept and pickled aboard the *Monongahela*.

Soon afterwards the two whalers separated – the *Rebecca Sims* headed for home, while the *Monongahela* and its unique cargo set off for the Arctic. The *Monongahela* was not seen again. About ten years later a party of eskimos off Alaska found the only trace – the nameplate of the doomed ship. What the creature was remains a mystery.

The armour-plated Chiton mollusc can live up to four kilometres below the surface of the ocean. It has up to 11,500 eyes!

The Great Barrier Reef, off the east coast of Australia, is the longest coral reef in the world, extending for over 2,000 kilometres.

In February 1948 an SOS was sent from a Dutch freighter, the *Ourang Medan*, which was in the Pacific on its way to Indonesia. The message said: 'Captain and all officers aboard dead. Entire crew dead or dying.' When rescuers reached the ship, they found all the officers in the chart room. All were dead – it seemed they had died within seconds of one another. Their eyes stared in horror and their arms were set, pointing upwards! On deck, dead men lay where they had fallen. There was no sign of disease, asphyxiation or poison on the bodies. What caused this sudden wave of death aboard the ship remains unknown.

The remora, or sucker fish, has a sucker on top of its head, which it attaches to a shark or whale. The fish then eats the leftovers from the host. Sometimes the remora can end up in the shark or whale's mouth, where it will wait for food to come along.

 Unlike most fishes, whales and sharks cannot swim backwards.

The eggs of a sea horse hatch inside a pocket on the father's belly.

 Penguins can swim fast enough underwater to allow them to leap two metres or more into the air and on to land or ice.

The octopus has three hearts.

 The world's largest crab is found in deep seas off Japan. It is known as the Japanese spider crab and it has the largest leg span of any arthropod, reaching up to 3.8 metres (12 feet) across! It can live for up to 100 years.

One of the most unusual underwater explorers is the dog Hooch, owned by Sean Herbert. Hooch first went into the sea when she followed her master one day – and liked it. Over a few years Hooch became a real explorer. Sean bought her her own £700 scuba outfit and she made 14 underwater dives! Hooch also took to the air, making 53 parachute jumps. She had to retire when she broke her leg – jumping off her master's bed!

 A sea horse can move each eye in a different direction at the same time.

Humpback whales can be heard at a distance of 1,200 kilometres – the distance between London and Barcelona, Spain.

Native divers in the Pacific will dive to depths of up to 37 metres – the height of a 14-storey building – for pearls. The pressure at this depth is up to five times that of the pressure on land. The divers can stay down for about three minutes.

During a trip in 1966, the *San Pueblo*, a US Navy research vessel, came across an awesome sight off Newfoundland, Canada. A sperm whale, some 18 metres long, was throwing itself out of the sea in an attempt to escape the tentacles of a giant squid said to be just as long!

 When young, a barnacle has three pairs of legs and one eye. It becomes even stranger as it gets older – gaining another eye and two more legs and then losing its mouth!

 Experiments show that the squid is attracted by the colour red. It seems that many of the survivors from ships sunk in World War II were doomed because they wore bright red life jackets.

 The starfish is the only animal able to turn its stomach inside out.

The gannet, a large seabird, eats so much that it is sometimes unable to fly.

The bottom of the ocean remains the most unexplored area of the world – so far only about 1.5 per cent of the seabed has been looked at in detail.

 King penguins are said to fall backwards in surprise on seeing humans.

 The deepest life form isn't in the sea, or even at the bottom of the sea, but under the floor of the sea! A type of bacteria has been found 842 metres below the seabed in the Woodlark Basin in the Pacific Ocean off New Guinea!

 Squid communicate with each other by changing colour.

Devastating Dinosaurs

Among the statues found near the village of Preambero, Mexico, in 1945, were models of dinosaurs. They were dated to the Mesozoic era – up to 65,000 years ago. But there were supposed to be no dinosaurs alive at that time! Why the models were made remains a mystery.

The word 'dinosaur' was first used at Plymouth in July 1841 at a meeting of the British Association for the Advancement of Science.

The reason why the Siberian mammoths found in glaciers did not decompose is because the ice they were surrounded by had antiseptic properties, which preserved their flesh, hair and everything else.

Among the most common fossils are those of snails. They may never have gone far. Today's average snail will take 115 days to travel a mile.

Charles Darwin became famous for finding out how all types of creatures can evolve and possibly survive in a changing environment. This made sense of the idea of dinosaurs.

In 1973, an American scientist, John Ostrom, showed that there was a connection between bird fossils and dinosaurs. He suggested that birds may have come directly from dinosaur ancestors.

Not all dinosaurs were big. The compsognathus dinosaur, a lizard-like creature with long back legs and little front legs, was about the size of a bicycle wheel.

Footprints show that dinosaurs were able to move rapidly.

During the Dark Ages, scientists in Italy believed that fossils were freaks of nature and that the animals never existed.

Over the years there have been many theories about why dinosaurs died out – one said they died off because they were bored!

There are a small number of 'living fossils' – creatures thought to have died out with the dinosaurs which have been rediscovered. A live coelacanth, an ancient fish of the deep ocean, was found in 1938.

There is evidence that a huge meteorite hit the earth 65 million years ago and wiped out the dinosaurs. In August 1991 Dr Jack Wolfe found fossils in the Teapot Dome, Wyoming, USA, which seemed to prove this happened.

Close to the centre of Glasgow, in Victoria Park, there are the remains of an ancient petrified forest.

A unique dinosaur, called tinysaurus, was found in Italy in 1998. It was very special. It was a baby relative of the fearsome Tyrannosaurus rex, and was the best preserved of all dinosaurs. Even its insides were preserved! The baby was probably 3–4 weeks old and showed all its muscles and a tiny tummy. A model based on the fossil showed it looked like a big lizard, with sharp claws and long back feet. There was something else unusual about this tiddler. It was the first dinosaur found in Italy. Because Italy was under water 113 million years ago, nearly all dinosaur remains had rotted in the sea. This baby was only preserved because it was quickly covered in sand and no bacteria attacked the dead body.

It is possible that the first creature on land was an ancestor of present-day insects – a 430-million-year-old fossil was found in western Australia.

For over 300 years fossil fuels have driven the world. The remains of ancient creatures and plants, which have been compressed into solids, like coal, and liquids, like oil, provide the majority of the power of modern industry.

There is no sure way of finding out how old a dinosaur is. The ages of dinosaurs are based on good guesses.

In 1998 it was found that the ancestors of the lion, elephant, rabbit and horse were around at the time of the dinosaurs, 70–100 million years ago.

The ages of early life and of the dinosaurs have been given names:

Cambrian. The time of simple sea life and plants. 570 million years ago.

Ordovician. The time of sea life and the first land life including snails. 500 million years ago.

Silurian. The time of animals with backbones, and leafless plants on land. 440 million years ago.

Devonian. The time of bony fishes and winged creatures that came ashore. 395 million years ago.

Carboniferous. The time of amphibious reptiles. Creatures with legs. 340 million years ago.

Permian. The time of more reptiles and larger land and sea life. About 275 million years ago.

Triassic. The time of the first dinosaurs, with two and
four legs. The first mammals. 225 million years ago.

Jurassic. The time of the great dinosaurs, the first birds
and a host of shellfish, including ammonites, in the
sea. About 195 million years ago.

Cretaceous. The time of the pterodactyl, the giant
lizards and the first warm-blooded animals. 136
million years ago.

Tertiary. The time the dinosaurs and large marine
reptiles disappeared and the ancestors of modern
animals arrived. 50–100 million years ago.

◯ The present-day alligator gives some idea of
how noisy life among the dinosaurs would
have been. The present alligator's bellow
can be heard up to a mile away.

◯ Dinosaurs preferred warmer weather and often
moved great distances away from the cold.

◯ The remains of a complete mosquito from the
dinosaur era were found whole and trapped in amber
in a mine in Mexico in 1990. The story was used as the
opening for Spielberg's monster hit film *Jurassic Park*.

◯ High up on Big Hill in the mountains of Kentucky,
USA, the movement of wagons along the track
gradually broke the rock. By the 1880s the loose

stones were all over the place and it was decided to clear them up. When the surface was cleared, a layer of rock 300 million years old was found underneath. In it were preserved the prints of the feet of a large prehistoric bear and, amazingly, the tracks of a human being! The toes were well spread and there was little doubt the print was human. How what seemed to be 300 million-year-old human footprints turned up remains a mystery.

A pig-like creature, the long-nosed peccary, was supposed to have died out over 2 million years ago – but it was rediscovered in Paraguay, South America, in 1975!

Nearly one third of the entire history of the Earth can be seen in the layers of rock at the spectacular Grand Canyon in the USA. In 1924, in one of the strangest unexplained discoveries, an expedition led by Edward Doheny in the Hava Supai canyon near the Grand Canyon came across rock paintings showing a Tyrannosaurus rex and a stegosaurus and men attacking a mammoth!

In Moscow there is what is said to be the world's largest dinosaur claw – it is 70 centimetres long!

The oldest dinosaur eggs were found in 2004 in the Golden Gate Highlands National Park. They are believed to be 190 million years old.

After the ancient bird the pteranodon took off, using its giant 8-metre wings, it had to be careful. If it crashed in the sea, it had to wait until there was a strong enough wind before it could take off again.

In 1915 a German meteorologist noticed that the coastlines of North and South America seemed to fit together. This began the idea of continents drifting over millions of years. Though he was made fun of at the time, the idea that the land of the Earth was once all joined together and slowly drifted apart is now accepted. This theory explained why similar dinosaur remains have been found in different continents and revealed that the position of the seas has changed over millions of years.

The ancient croc, the grandaddy of them all, is known as the 'horror crocodile'. It lived in what is now southern USA and Mexico about 75 million years ago. It grew up to 15 metres and its head alone was 2 metres long!

The largest dinosaur was probably the diplodocus ('double beam'), which grew to 27 metres long – the length of two buses!

One type of prehistoric turtle was as big as a fully-grown man.

The egg of the aepyornis, a prehistoric bird, is the largest ever. It held around 11 litres of yolk and white – enough for hundreds of breakfasts.

The largest prehistoric land mammal was the giant ancestor of the rhino – it stood 8 metres from head to foot.

William Buckland, an English clergyman who made many discoveries about fossils in the 19th century, was very strange. He liked eating as many different things as possible, and his diet included garden snails, crocodile meat and bats. People were always able to identify him – wherever he went he carried a feather duster.

The fossil of an ancestor of the horse revealed that it was about the size of a rabbit – only 25–50 cm high – and had an arched back.

◯ Minute fossils, which can only be seen under a microscope, have been preserved all over the world. Fossil lumps of the super-hard tiny ocean creatures called diatoms are still sold as an abrasive (like sandpaper) known as 'tripoli powder'.

◯ The English fossil hunter and botanist Charles Lyell became the first to prove the biblical story of history was not an accurate picture of the story of the Earth. His ideas were supported by the Archbishop of Canterbury and the Bishop of London.

◯ Dinosaurs were many shapes and sizes. Here are some of them . . .

Brontosaurus. 25–30 metres long. 30 tons. 159m years ago.

Megalosaurus. Flesh eater. 6 metres. 190–140m years.

Denoychus. 3 metres. 140m years.

Iguanodon. 12 metres. 4 tons. 104m years.

Acanthopholis. Plant eater. 4 metres. 100m years.

Triceratops. Plant eater. 7 metres. 70m years.

Protoceratops. Plant eater. 2 metres. 90m years.

Cerotopsian. 8 metres. 10 tons. 90m years.

◯ The two first major US dinosaur hunters, Marsh and Cope, didn't get on – they named the most horrible dinosaurs they found after each other!

William J. Meister, out looking for fossils in Utah with his wife and two daughters in June 1968, made a spectacular find. William split open a rock and found inside what looked like the print of a sandal. Beside it was a crushed trilobite, an ancient fossil sea creature like today's horseshoe crab. The trilobites had died out about 280 million years before! Scientists could not accept the man was alive then, but they could give no explanation for the print.

Many fossils now need to be preserved, not only from the weather, but from people. In the 1980s vandals destroyed some of the most ancient humanoid footprints, found on rock at a farm in Kentucky in 1938. The rock itself was exceptionally old – dating from 250 million years ago!

The stegosaurus, weighing about 1.9 tonnes, had a brain the size of a walnut – just 70 grammes.

One of the biggest collections of dinosaur eggs was discovered in the Pyrenean mountains, on the border of France and Spain. There were about 30,000 of them.

During the period of the dinosaurs and the time that followed, the beginnings of modern animals appeared. Among them were:

The titanothere – hippopotamus

The miacid – cat

The tomarctus – dog

The entelodont – pig (this one was a bit big, though, being almost as high as a man!)

The oxydactylus – a mix between a giraffe and a camel!

The sabre-toothed tiger – tiger

The izard – chamois, a type of horned antelope

When Victorian fossil hunter Sir Richard Owen put together the fossil of the bird archaeopteryx, the wings were upside down – according to him, the bird flew backstroke!

Forget about counting the teeth of fossil sea snails or slugs – they can have up to 750,000 of them!

Dinosaur names – what do they mean?

Brontosaurus – thunder lizard

Ichthyosaurus – fish lizard

Pterodactyl – finger-winged

Archaeopteryx – ancient-winged

Theriomorph – in the form of a beast

Gigantosaurus – great lizard

Oviraptor – egg stealer

In August 1966, the pygmy opossum was found in Australia – it had been believed extinct and had only previously been known by 20,000-year-old fossils.

In September 1997 Canada sent the 75-million-year-old skeleton of the dinosaur ihypocrasaurus, which had taken two years to put together, to The Hague, Holland, for the opening of the film *The Lost World*. Soon after it arrived workers dropped it, smashing it to bits!

The first dinosaur fossil was discovered by accident. In March 1822, on a Sussex road near Lewes, Mary Mantell, waiting for her doctor husband to finish a visit to a patient, found a fossil tooth among rocks being used for road-mending.

The first dinosaur tracks were found way before full fossils. In 1802 an American boy, Pliny Moody, discovered the first tracks near South Hadley in Massachusetts.

A disaster seems to have led to the evolution of the dinosaurs about 248 million years ago when 98% of all marine animals and many small animals died out.

Dinosaur skin is rare. The fossil skin that has been found is very varied, with spikes, scales and patterns.

It was the English anatomist Richard Owen who named the dinosaur, using the Greek words *deinos* (terrible) and *sauros* (lizard).

Cambridge geologist Dr Edward Clarke gave himself a shock in 1818. He was looking for fossils in a chalk quarry when he reached a layer some 80 metres down. He came across the fossils of ancient sea urchins and newts. Noticing that three of the newts were complete specimens, he dug them out carefully. Taking them home, he separated the fossil newts from the rock around them and put them on a sheet of paper in the sun. The newts soon began to move! Within a short time two of the newts died, but the third remained alive. Dr Clarke put this survivor in a pond, but it soon escaped. Nothing could shake the doctor's belief that these newts were fossils, had been extinct and yet had come back to life!

The smartest dinosaur – the troodon – only lived in North America. It had huge eyes and a brain equal to that of modern mammals and birds. A troodon hand had three fingers and could grasp objects. The third toe on its back feet was used to slash its prey.

The deadliest dinosaur, the deinonychus, which had sickle-shaped claws, was limited to a small area – fossils have only been found in western USA.

Some dinosaurs appear to have hunted in great herds – so many that they stretched as far as the eye could see. One grave in Montana contained the remains of 10,000 duckbill maiasauras! It seems that large herds did have problems – they often trod on each other's tails, breaking them.

In January 1983, William Walker discovered a huge fossil claw bone in a Surrey clay pit – it was a curved claw about 30 cm long. It turned out to be the most important European dinosaur discovery of the 20th century – the baryonyx. It took three weeks for the skeleton to be dug out and the discovery was only officially announced in November 1986.

Groups of female protoceratops dinosaurs laid their eggs together – in nests where the group of eggs was bigger than a single full-grown dinosaur!

There were 6 million years between dinosaurs and the appearance of people.

The only remains of dinosaurs having a fight were found in Mongolia. A protoceratops and a velociraptor were hit by a sandstorm and died fighting.

'Living' fossils are present-day creatures which go back millions of years:

Dragonflies. They first appeared 320 million years ago.

Cockroaches. These insects appeared about 200 million years ago.

Crocodiles. They first appeared some 90 million years ago.

Coelacanth. This fish first appeared some 390 million years ago.

Turtles. They first appeared some 10 million years ago.

Tortoises. They first appeared some 12 million years ago.

In ancient China dinosaur bones were thought to be the remains of dragons – they were ground up for medicines and magic potions.

During work to excavate a railway tunnel for the St Dizier to Nancy railway line in France in 1856, a group of workmen came across a prehistoric limestone boulder blocking their way forward. In the half-light, the men began to split the rock with their hammers and pickaxes. Slowly the rock split and began to fall apart. To their amazement they saw a creature inside – a pterodactyl, with a wingspan of over three metres. Even more astounding, the creature fluttered its wings, croaked and died! This living fossil had four legs and its wings were like those of a bat. Where it would have had feet were long talons. Its mouth had a row of sharp teeth. The skin was leathery, thick and oily. The now dead fossil was taken to the nearby town of Gray and confirmed as a pterodactyl. The rock in which the creature had apparently hibernated was four million years old! This almost unbelievable story was widely reported in February that year, and was printed, with pictures, in London.

Like in trees, there are growth rings in dinosaur bones.

When the first fossils were found in Europe in the 17th century, it was thought they could be dated by licking them! If they had a lot of jelly (or gelatine) in them then they couldn't be that old. Just to check, people then looked at how many black specks the bones had. If they had lots, then they were ancient. These methods turned out to be entirely useless.

The world's most ancient living fossils were discovered by chance in 1972 in a laboratory deep in the Ural Mountains in Russia. A scientist was experimenting with a piece of the ore of the metal potassium. He wanted to find out why it was coloured red. He prepared slides of small flakes of the rock and looked at them under a microscope. Among the flakes he noticed tiny organisms. Since these often turned up in ancient rock, he wasn't bothered. When he finished, he popped them into a solution in a flask. Several days later he had another look at the solution. The flask was now swarming with living microscopic creatures! In later experiments he was able to see them grow and reproduce. He was astounded – for these tiny organisms had been trapped in rock for 250 million years.

It is estimated that the mouth of a fully-grown Tyrannosaurus rex could hold enough food for a human family for a month.

The skins of dinosaurs have been found mummified in the cold dry air of Patagonia, South America.

You too can eat dinosaur food. The ginkgo tree, which first appeared in the Jurassic age, is still with us – a number of them grow in Britain. Other plants from the dinosaur age still grow today. One plant from Canada, eaten by veggie dinosaurs, is sold in cans for salads!

Sap from trees can solidify as yellow or red amber. When insects were caught in it during the age of the dinosaurs, even the soft body parts were preserved.

One of the first collectors of fossils in Britain was John Conyers. He was an antique dealer and chemist who lived in the 17th century. He was digging under old buildings in Gray's Inn Lane, London, when he came across a jumble of ancient bones. He claimed, correctly, they were the fossils of ancient elephants. Everyone thought he was daft. They said it was too cold for elephants to have lived in Britain! A friend said they must have been elephants kept in a zoo by the Romans.

The brother of the early woman fossil hunter Mary Anning found the fossil of a large marine reptile by Lyme Regis beach in 1810 when he was 11. A year later, he and his sister found a 10-metre-long ichthyosaurus. The discovery caused immense excitement. Mary is still remembered today with the tongue-twister 'She sells seashells on the seashore'.

The Tyrannosaurus rex did not eat with its fingers – its front legs were too short to reach its mouth.

While the Loch Ness monster is the most famous of the 'living creatures' said to have survived from the age of the dinosaurs, there are plenty of others. In Canada, an unknown creature has been sighted on the Okanagan Lake. It is called Ogopogo. In July 1968, five water-skiers, aged between 14 and 21, were on the lake when they saw a strange sight. A long shape appeared in the water only 6 metres from the group. It had blue-green scales and glistened in the sun. Soon it sped off across the lake, ahead of their motorboat which was going at 40 miles an hour! It then disappeared.

Walter Granger of Columbia University in New York was sent in 1897 to find new dinosaurs. He went off to Wyoming, but found that all the good fossils seemed to have been dug up already. One day he walked across a plain towards a shepherd's shack. When he reached it, he was astounded. The cabin was built from the giant dinosaur bones, which were all around it! He started digging and soon found a huge number of fossils in 'Bone Cabin Quarry'. The huge brontosaurus now on display in New York is one of his finds.

The great English scientist Darwin discovered mammal fossils during his famous voyage on the HMS *Beagle*. These helped give him the idea of evolution.

Spectacular Space

 During a May night in 1994, Uganda was hit by at least 863 lumps of meteorite. Luckily, only one boy was injured and a banana tree broke the fall of the lump that hit him.

 The tiny neutron star, left over when a star collapses, is so heavy that a piece the size of a pinhead would weigh as much as a supertanker.

 The longest recorded solar eclipse was on January 15 2010. It lasted 11 minutes, 7.8 seconds.

 Major Titov of the USSR is the youngest person so far to have gone into space, at the age of 25 years and 329 days.

 A black and white teddy bear, Mishka, went into space aboard the Soviet Salyut 6 in 1979. Mishka was the first teddy bear to orbit the earth.

 The Hubble space telescope was launched on April 24 1990.

The three words spoken at the launch of the first US manned rocket, on May 5 1961, were not what you might think. They were: 'Ignition . . . Mainstage . . . Lift-off.'

 Space is a funny environment. If an average person stays weightless in space for 4.5 months they will lose about 12 per cent or one eighth of their pelvic bone. In time, fluid will also get into the brain, making the head foggy, so that it becomes impossible to think straight. At the moment, if someone travelled to Mars, the loss of calcium in their bones would be so great that by the time they arrived they would only be able to crawl!

 Phobos, the Soviet probe orbiting Mars, disappeared in 1989. It was claimed it had been intercepted by Martians!

 It is estimated that the sun weighs 330,000 times as much as the earth.

 The planet Neptune was first found in 1795, but at the time it was thought to be just another star. It was re-discovered in 1846.

In April 1968 an agreement was signed by many countries, including Britain, the USA and the then Soviet Union, to rescue any astronauts in trouble.

When astronauts shave in space they use razors with a vacuum attachment so that the bristles do not float about in the capsule.

On the planet Mercury, a day is two-thirds the length of a year. It takes just under 88 days for the planet to revolve around the sun and 58.6 days for it to revolve around its own axis.

 Nearly a quarter of the world's population watched American astronaut Neil Armstrong take the first human step on the moon on July 20 1969. At first, Mission Control were frightened that he would sink into the moon-dust, but they needn't have worried. The lack of gravity meant that his footsteps were only three millimetres deep and that his backpack, which had weighed 227 kg back on Earth, weighed only 45 kg on the moon!

The toilet for the space shuttle Endeavour cost £19.5 million to build.

 The features of the moon of planet Uranus are all named after characters from Shakespeare's plays.

 Light travels at a speed of nearly 10 billion kilometres a year.

 The craters on the planet Mercury are named after great artists, musicians and writers, including Van Gogh, Matisse, Beethoven, Wagner and Milton.

 The fastest man-made vehicle is the Ulysses space probe which travels at 27.4 miles per second.

 On their first trip to the moon, the Americans left a tribute to the astronauts who died in Apollo 1 and to the two Soviet cosmonauts Yuri Gagarin and Vladimir Komarov. They also left a golden olive branch to symbolize peace.

 Boiling and freezing take place at the same temperature in space.

In 1456 Pope Calixtus III declared that Halley's comet was an agent of the Devil and excommunicated it!

Small craters on Venus are named after famous women including Florence Nightingale.

Some important dates in space:

1957. The first satellite (Sputnik) is launched by Russia.

1959. Manned rockets are proposed in the USA.

1960 (May). A dummy astronaut is launched by the Russians.

1961 (April). Yuri Gagarin of Russia becomes the first man in space.

1961 (May). Alan Shepard becomes the first American in space.

1962 (July). The first satellite TV is introduced.

1965. Two Soviet cosmonauts walk in space.

1969 (July). The first men land on the moon.

1970. The first Chinese satellite is launched.

1970. The first Japanese satellite is launched.

1971 (December). The first craft lands on Mars.

1972 (July). The first craft lands on Venus.

1976. The first US spacecraft lands on Mars and takes photos.

1990 (April). The Hubble space telescope is launched.

1997 (July). The Mars Pathfinder lands.

The most dramatic of space ventures took place in 1970. On April 13, Mission Control in Houston, USA, lost communication with Apollo 13 for two seconds. No one noticed. But just after 9.00 that day, the three astronauts noticed a yellow alarm flash and a shudder moved through the craft. An explosion had taken place in one of the fuel tanks and two fuel cells were out. Astronaut Jim Swigert signalled back to Earth with the words 'Houston, we have a problem'. The spacecraft began to wobble and the planned moon landing was quickly abandoned. Houston realized that the craft was losing power and the oxygen supply was beginning to fall. Apollo 13 was over 300,000 miles from Earth. After moving into the lunar module, the astronauts were able to fire the engine in an attempt to return to Earth. For two tense days, the attention of the world was on the three men. They went without sleep, and put together a way of keeping oxygen in the cold module. Eventually, they were able to fire the engine for re-entry to the earth's atmosphere. To everyone's relief, they made it.

When the US Apollo X re-entered the earth's atmosphere in 1969, it was travelling at 24,790.8 miles an hour – faster than man had ever flown before.

The chimps that the Americans sent into space have their own retirement home and park in California.

 In 1980 it was found that cosmonauts Leonid Popov and Valery Ryumin had grown three centimetres during their record 185-day space flight.

 The range of temperature for a Martian day runs from -30 to -86°C.

A meteor, believed to be a relic from near the time of creation, hit the earth's atmosphere in June 1998. It was reported as a UFO by people from Devon to North Wales.

Twelve people at Mission Control, Houston, had to give the go-ahead for the moon landing in 1969. Everyone said 'Go'. If someone had said 'No go', then man would not have gone on to land on the moon.

A colour picture of the whole universe can now be put together by images taken from a radio telescope. It's a pretty picture because the colours change as the amount of radiation in the universe changes. The red parts show the centre of the universe.

 Lumps of odd rock and debris, known as asteroids, collect around the larger planets. Those near Jupiter travel at up to 60,000 miles an hour.

 Pluto is 5,914 million kilometres from the sun.

 The words 'The eagle has landed' were spoken on the moon in July 1969. The Eagle was the name of the small craft that had landed on the moon.

 An explosion on the sun, called a blinker, is equivalent to the explosion of 100 tons of dynamite.

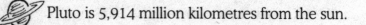 The planet Neptune and its moon were discovered by the English brewer and part-time stargazer William Lassell, in 1846.

A sunquake has enough energy to power the USA for 20 years. The average sunquake is 10,000 times as strong as the huge San Francisco earthquake of 1906.

On November 3 1957, the Soviet dog Leika became the first animal in space. Two mice were the next animals in space. They were sent up in a US rocket on December 13 1958.

One of the messages sent into space on the Voyager 2 craft was in Latin, the language of Ancient Rome. It said, 'Greetings to you, wherever you are; we have good will towards you and bring peace across space.' The Chinese message was a bit different: 'Hope everyone's well. We are thinking about you all. Please come here to visit us when you have time.' So, when aliens do turn up on your doorstep, remember, they were invited!

 1,300 Earths can fit into the planet Jupiter.

 The world's largest meteorite was discovered on a farm in South Africa. Known as the Hoba West, it weighs a terrific 54.4 tonnes and measures 2.73 metres by 2.43 metres – even after one million years out in the sun and rain!

A flight of the US space shuttle was once held up by a woodpecker, who decided that the nose cone would be a suitable object to peck. The dozy bird was eventually persuaded to go away.

 The moon is thought to have separated from the earth about 3,000 million years ago.

 A comet which appeared over Italy in 1347 was described as a black star and was said to foretell doom. The Black Death arrived in Europe within months.

 Helen Sharman, the first British astronaut, was 27 when she took off from Russia in the Soyuz TM 12 on May 19 1991. She was subsidized by à Moscow bank. The cost of her trip was said to be £5 million.

 A rocket has to travel at over 17,450 miles an hour to leave the earth's atmosphere and not be dragged back by gravity.

 In space, bread dries out. Tortillas are carried on the space shuttle instead.

Britain's largest telescope, the 20-centimetre Great Equatorial Refractor telescope, was installed at the Old Royal Observatory, Greenwich, in 1893.

The nearest star to the sun is called Proxima Centauri. It is a mere 34 billion kilometres away!

The Russians sent all sorts of living things into space in the 1960s – plants, insects, frogs, rabbits, guinea pigs and dogs.

On the Apollo 8 mission of 1968, the US astronauts James Lovell, Frank Borman and William Anders were the first people to see the dark side of the moon.

It may seem incredible, but iron on the moon does not rust. Samples of the iron brought back by both the American and Russian expeditions have remained rust-free for years.

It takes 8 minutes and 38 seconds for the sun's rays to reach the earth, so at the moment we look at it, it is not actually where we see it, but has travelled a bit relative to us.

On January 7 1610, Galileo of Italy became the first to see the three moons of Jupiter. His work was considered heresy by the Church, since he supported the idea that the planets move around the sun. As a result he was confined to his home from 1633 to 1641, after a trial by the Inquisition of the Catholic Church.

 Greenwich observatory was established in 1676.

 In the Somali language, a satellite is 'a star that failed to reach Heaven'.

 Water was found on the moon by the US lunar prospector probe in March 1998. There was enough water there to support up to 10,000 two-person households for over 100 years!

 Halley discovered the comet named after him in 1682, confirming that it had appeared in 1607 and 1531. He did not live long enough to see it again in 1757.

 The temperature of Pluto is approximately -220°C.

 French physicist Armand Fizeau discovered the speed of light in 1849. It is about 300,000 kilometres an hour.

In 1687 the astronomer Edmund Halley paid for Newton's work on the laws of gravity to be published.

 Lieutenant James Cook (later Captain Cook) was sent to Tahiti in 1768 to set up an observatory so that the planet Venus's movement across the sun could be seen.

 In 1781 William Herschel discovered the planet Uranus when using a home-made telescope in his garden in Bath. It was the first new planet to be discovered for 4,000 years, since Babylonian prehistory.

 As the Eagle was coming in to land on the moon for the first time ever, astronauts Neil Armstrong and Buzz Aldrin found that their computer had failed. They were guided down by speaking to the Houston space centre.

 When a massive star collapses and explodes, it is called a supernova. A huge amount of energy is released when this happens. In recorded human history only two supernovas are known of. One was seen in 1604 and another on February 23 1987, by a 30-year-old Canadian, Ian

Skelton. He was using an old telescope at the mountain observatory of Las Campanas, Chile, when he photographed the supernova.

 The spacesuit worn by the first man on the moon, Neil Armstrong, had six layers. It was extremely light.

 There are 400 billion stars in the Milky Way.

 To test how well their hearts work, astronauts have to lie head down on a very sloping table for 25 minutes.

 In June 1983, Valentina Tereshkova of Russia became the first woman in space.

 On August 21 1995, NASA's expensive Mars Observer vanished as it approached Mars.

 The first person recorded as having been injured by a meteorite was Mrs Ann Hodges of Sylacauga in Alabama, USA, on November 30 1954. A 4 kg meteorite crashed through the roof of her house and hit her on the arm and bruised her hip.

The word meteor comes from an Ancient Greek word that means 'things in the air'.

 Only five or six of the 500 or so meteorites which fall on the earth each year are found.

On December 6 1993, Tom Akers set a new US record with a space walk of 22 hours, 50 minutes from the space shuttle Endeavour, beating the previous record by a minute. His co-astronaut, Kathy Thornton, set a new female record of 14 hours, 12 minutes.

 The Mars Polar Lander space mission of 1998 was unusual: on board was a CD-ROM with the names of one million children from all over the world.

 On a mission to Mars, people would have to be sheltered from four types of rays: cosmic rays, the rays of the Van Allen radiation belts, nuclear rays and giant solar flares. Their water – for washing and drinking – would also have to be protected so it did not turn radioactive.

When Galileo used his early telescopes in the 17th century, the best he could do was magnify things by twenty.

 By 2011, 55 women had flown in space. 45 were American, 3 Soviet/Russian, 2 Canadian, 2 Japanese, 1 French, 1 South Korean and 1 British – Helen Sharman.

 It is reckoned that the force of the asteroid that made the huge crater in Arizona was equivalent to that of 800 atom bombs.

 In 1961 the US Post Office introduced 'speed mail' – messages sent by satellite. They were printed out on earth and delivered. E-mail has now replaced this system.

 Telstar 1, a satellite launched in July 1962, made international TV possible for the first time. It also made long-distance phone calls easier.

 One of the tests early astronauts had to undertake was to plunge their feet in ice-cold water, then spend two hours in a room at a temperature of 54°C.

We are still here . . . just. Satellites are not always perfect. In September 1983, the world could have been blown up by nuclear weapons. A Russian Cosmos satellite went wrong that day and sent a message to Earth saying that the United States had launched nuclear missiles which were on their way to Russia. A smart Russian soldier decided that the satellite had made a mistake and quickly told the authorities not to launch the Russian missiles. They agreed it was a fault. Phew!

 In 1565, when aged nineteen, the great Danish astronomer Tycho Brahe lost his nose in a fight. He then wore a false nose made of silver and gold which he stuck on with cement – a pot of which he always carried around with him, just in case. He was later given an island to work from by King Frederick II of Denmark.

The Mars Pathfinder expedition of 1997 discovered that ancient Mars had been wet and possibly able to support life.

Anaxagorus, a Greek philosopher who died in 428 BC, was condemned for the weird idea he had that the sun was a molten rock measuring 100 miles across which glowed with super-heat, instead of a flat disc in the sky. Of course he was right – apart from the size.

 Close to dawn on June 30 1908, a huge flash was seen in the sky and a loud bang was heard over the thick forests of the remote area of Tunguska, Siberia. Villagers up to two hundred miles away fled in terror. A number of people were badly burned or thrown through the air as a massive fireball hurtled to Earth. For some 40 miles from the centre of the event, the trees were blown down in patterns showing the direction of the blast. Scientists only reached the remote spot years later, in 1927. They found no tell-tale signs of a meteorite impact or a crater. The cause remains a mystery, though it is likely it was a comet which exploded just above the earth. The ice and dust would have left no visible evidence.

The first observatory was established in Nuremberg in 1471. The astronomer who designed it saw Halley's comet the next year.

The first nebula (constellation of stars), Andromeda, was recorded as early as 963 by the Arabian Al Sufi.

 The earth is surrounded by a ring of dust.

Awesome Aliens

 A very old carving by the Maya Indians in Mexico seems to show a man inside a spaceship, using some form of controls. It is said to be a picture of a visit from outer space over 1,000 years ago!

A statue made over one thousand years ago in central Europe is very strange – it shows a figure in something like a spacesuit with antennae.

In the year 1211 a ship in the sky was seen by people outside a church in Ireland. It was said that the anchor of this fantastic airship was kept in the church for a long time.

The famous Ancient Greek Aristotle reported seeing 'heavenly discs' in the sky over Greece. The Roman historian Pliny said his UFOs looked like 'a burning shield' which had sparks. He had probably seen part of a meteorite shower.

A large silver disc was sighted by the Abbot and monks of Bagland Abbey, Yorkshire, in 1290.

In a monastery in Yugoslavia there are pictures of flying objects with creatures inside. They were painted in the Middle Ages!

During May 1909, people in over forty towns in Britain and New Zealand reported seeing UFOs. One person who saw them said he had a close encounter with two aliens near his home in Wales. He said the spaceship that took off was a large cylinder-shaped object.

The famous English sailor and airman Francis Chichester reported what was probably the first UFO seen from an aircraft He was flying south of Australia in 1931 when he saw a strange object in the sky.

The man who looked after the Royal Air Force in Britain during World War II, Lord Dowding, believed flying saucers existed though he never saw one himself. He received many reports of UFOs from airmen flying planes during the war.

Over 850 UFOs were reported in America in June and July 1947.

The first reports of a UFO crash near Roswell, New Mexico, were made in July 1947. One of the witnesses was a Captain Henderson. He said he was sent in a B-29 plane to recover the crashed bits of the spaceship. These and any of the alien crew were to go to the Wright Field air base, California. He said the aliens were 'little people with exceptionally large heads'.

 US astronauts James McDivitt and Ed White said they saw a silver cylindrical object when orbiting the Earth in 1965. Houston control centre said it was a piece of space junk, but the astronauts still believed they had seen a UFO.

 A netball teacher, Bronwen Williams, and nine children were playing a game of netball at their school at Anglesey, when they saw a UFO. Afterwards Bronwen Williams asked each of the children to draw what they had seen. They all drew a cigar-shaped craft with a black dome.

Some famous people have seen UFOs. The former United States President Jimmy Carter said he saw one in 1973. When he became President, he could not forget his interest. He launched a $20m study into UFOs.

The pilots of a Pan Am plane reported seeing six red-coloured UFOs in 1952. They were about five metres across and their speed was about 10,000 miles an hour.

By 1990, over 100,000 people had claimed to have seen UFOs.

Salesman Alan Cave claimed that he had an encounter with an alien when he was out driving in the West Country in 1981. Afterwards he found that he could not account for two hours, and that the number on his car's milometer had gone down by 300!

 In December 1978, John Day, aged 33, drove into a strange green mist in Essex, England. He found he lost three hours of his life. Under hypnosis he said he had been abducted by three aliens, over two metres tall, who had pink eyes. When the aliens let him go, he was allowed to look round the UFO.

A family from Gloucester seem to have been abducted by aliens in June 1978. As they drove towards the top of a hill, they saw a white light in the sky. They heard a noise, and a huge saucer-like object approached.

They could not remember anything else. They just drove home. There they phoned the police and told them about the UFO. They realized there was an hour missing from their journey. Over the next few days the family were affected by itchy skin and strange bruises. The parents went to a hypnotist .When in a deep sleep, they said the family had been abducted by aliens from a planet called Janos.The aliens said they could share their secrets in return for a place to live on Earth. Doctors and scientists checked the story. They decided the parents believed they were telling the truth about what happened during that missing hour.

A police chief in Falkville, Alabama, in the USA was called to investigate a UFO. He said that he tracked the alien and took photographs of it, and that it had a suit like tin foil.

American Richard Price says that on an evening in September 1955, when he was eight years old, he came across two aliens in a cemetery at Troy, New York. They took him aboard their craft and injected an implant under his skin. Before he left the craft the aliens said he was to leave it alone, or he would die. At school in 1964, he told a friend about the aliens and everyone in the school called him 'the spaceman'. One day, in June 1989, while getting dressed, the 'implant' started to show. In August it came out. A scientist looked at it and said it looked like human skin but wasn't.

 Two small children in the USA were said to have been abducted by aliens and then returned to their beds in 1993. Each had strange orange blobs on their skin. When scientists looked at the blobs, they said they could not have been caused by anything in their house.

 In a strange case in 1966, two small boys discovered the bodies of two Brazilian TV workers in the hills near Rio. Beside the bodies were pieces of green and blue paper. One of the papers had a formula written on it. No one could understand the formula. The police investigated, but they were unable to find any reason for the men's deaths. The two men had gone out to buy a car, but they had bought raincoats instead – even though the day was hot and sunny. The police inspector, who had looked into lots of stories of UFOs, said the two may have died after making contact with a UFO. The formula was locked in a police safe. Later, when the safe was opened, the piece of paper had vanished! PC Alan Godfrey claims he was abducted by aliens in West Yorkshire. Seeing bright lights ahead on the road, he stopped his car. He tried to report what he saw – a metal object – but his car radio did not work. So, to remember what it looked like, he did a drawing of the object. The next thing he knew he was in his car, further down the road, and the object had gone. Back at the police station he found he had 'lost' some time. Then he remembered hearing a voice in his head. He went to see a hypnotist. When under hypnosis he said he had been abducted by aliens from a spacecraft.

Early in 1977 in the bushes of a garden in England a twelve-year-old boy saw a figure in a white suit and a helmet with a visor. His mother came out and said the figure floated towards the house. She called a friend, who tried to chase it. Another friend called the police. When two policemen arrived, the figure suddenly disappeared.

In 1961 a forester in Karelia, Russia, came across a large crater on the bank of a lake. He sent for divers and scientists to look at the strange hole. After a search of the bank and the lake, it was thought a huge object had skidded there. In the crater was a strange green ice which could not be explained. The crater remains a mystery. One scientist who saw it said a UFO may have landed there.

Feathery matter was left by the flying saucers seen in Italy in the 1950s. It fell from the sky for two hours after the UFOs were seen, but disappeared if it touched the warm ground or the skin. When examined by scientists it was found to be an unusual sort of glass. It was called 'angel hair'.

Almost all the people who say they have been abducted by aliens have had strong electric shocks earlier in their lives, such as being struck by lightning.

In 1996, Jesse Long, an American who claimed he had been abducted by aliens as a boy, had an operation to remove an 'implant' at a hospital in Los Angeles. A clear triangular sliver was removed from the lower part of his right leg. When looked at by scientists, it was found to be glass.

The American Apollo 12 moonflight is said to have come across two UFOs, 132,000 miles out in space. One was in front and one behind the Apollo. One astronaut said they were 'very bright and seemed to be flashing at us'. On the same flight a very bright light appeared between the Apollo 12 and the Earth. The Earth seemed to disappear behind the light for about ten minutes, before the light vanished.

In 1970 a mysterious event happened to an American plane. An American Airlines 727 passenger plane was coming into Miami airport in Florida. At the airport it was seen by radar. Then, suddenly, the plane disappeared from the radar for ten minutes. Then it came back on the screen. The plane came in, landed and everyone was safe. The radar people told the crew that they had 'lost' the plane from their screens for ten minutes. The pilots were amazed, but checked the time on the plane and on their watches – they were wrong by ten minutes! They knew that the clocks and the watches had been correct, because they had checked the time twenty minutes before they were due to land. So there could be no mistake. What happened is still unexplained.

One of the strangest mysteries in the history of the British Army is said to have happened in August 1915. The First Fourth Norfolk regiment were marched into low cloud on Hill 60 in Turkey. They were never seen again. Many now say they were taken by aliens.

On 24 March 1964 Jim Templeton took a photograph of his daughter Elizabeth on the marshes near the Solway Firth in Scotland.

When he took the picture, the two of them were quite alone. When he had the film developed there was a humanoid, dressed in silver clothes, standing behind Elizabeth.

 In Arès, France, a safe landing spot for UFOs has been built. It is called the Ovniport.

 A guide to identifying aliens was published in America in 1995. It lists fifty sorts of extraterrestrials, describing them in detail, and features colour illustrations.

For the film *Alien*, the first alien was made the size of a man's fist.

 Huge asteroids, mostly lumps of frozen rock, hit the Earth every million years or so. One is thought to have hit the Gulf of Mexico off America some 65 million years ago and is said to be the reason why the dinosaurs were wiped out.

The Americans have saucer-shaped aircraft, known as UAVs – Uninhabited Aerial Vehicles – which have been reported as UFOs.

The chance of a place having alien life is worked out by using maths – the sum is called the Drake Equation.

The first search for life on other planets was made in 1960.

By 1980 over 5,000 pieces of space junk had fallen back to Earth.

Dreamland is the name given to the mysterious Area 51 in Nevada, USA. The place is a US Government research centre. Its existence was not admitted until 1995. It is said that the Americans are flying captured UFOs from the base.

In October 1996 a man from Dagenham, Essex, took out an insurance policy against being kidnapped by aliens.

The famous 'Philadelphia Experiment' by the US Navy is said to have taken place in 1943. It happened at the harbour of the city of Philadelphia and later out to sea. A ship and the crew were made to disappear. A force field of some sort was put on the ship, a destroyer, and a green mist came up and covered the ship. The ship was said to have appeared and disappeared. At sea, the same thing happened. However, some of the men did not return at once and had to be brought back slowly. There were reports that some men became ill and some died. Later, some of the crew vanished at home, walking in the street or just sitting in public

places, only to come back later. What happened to
them was unexplained.

 Where did it come from? A gold pendant
was found in South America and was over
1,000 years old. Strangely it looks very
much like a plane.

 The Scottish Centre for Alien Activity is at
Bonnybridge near Glasgow.

A close encounter between a British Airways jet
with 60 people on board and a UFO was reported
in 1996 on a flight to Milan. The UFO had bright
lights and came so close to the plane that the co-
pilot ducked. Nothing was seen on radar.

So many strange things were seen in the air over
Europe in the Middle Ages that the two leading
Emperors decided on laws against these 'Tyrants of
the Air'. These unknown beings were said to kidnap
people and take them away in the sky for a while.
When the people came back, no one liked them,
and they were all burned at the stake!

 The American air force, the USAF, has often said
that UFOs do not exist. What is odd, though, is that
they tell pilots what to do if they see UFOs!

The Mars rock on which life was believed to have been found in 1996 was discovered in the Allan Hills in Antarctica in 1984. It was part of a meteorite from Mars.

A scientific study of Unidentified Flying Objects by the American Air Force and the University of Colorado was published in 1968. Only a small number of the UFO reports were thought to be truly unexplained.

One night, while going home from their small church, a group of people in the town of Merkel in Texas, USA, heard a strange sound. Looking into the night, they were amazed to see a large object moving along the ground. They stood and stared as the object moved nearer. They all said it was an anchor. It was attached by a rope to an 'airship' which hovered above the town. After a while, a small man was seen coming down the rope. In a short time, he came down to the ground, looked at the group of people, then went back to the ship. The anchor was pulled up, and off the airship went into the night sky!

 The surface of Mars is so cold that human skin would freeze if out in the open.

The first study of flying objects which are seen in the sky was made in Japan over 750 years ago – in the year 1235!

In Detroit, the famous 'Motor City' of America, the police have special orders. They are told how to look after captured aliens. They are told that aliens might be female and male and should be kept apart. Detroit does not seem to want little aliens to appear by accident.

Ten famous films involving aliens:
1. *Close Encounters of the Third Kind*
2. *The War of the Worlds*
3. *Independence Day*
4. *Superman* (He is an alien from the planet Krypton.)
5. *E.T. The Extra-Terrestrial*
6. *Star Wars*
7. *The Empire Strikes Back*
8. *Return of the Jedi*
9. *Alien*
10. *The Invasion of the Body Snatchers*

A study by a doctor in the 1980s found that small specks of dirt or dust in the eyes can sometimes be mistaken for UFOs.

 There is a story of a UFO in ancient Egypt. It tells of a winter night when a circle of fire was seen in the clear night sky. This turned into a group of objects and the Pharaoh was told about this strange sight. He went out of doors with a group of soldiers to see. The 'fire circles' stayed so long that he decided to eat outside while he watched them. The lights went higher and higher in the sky until they disappeared. When they had gone, the Pharaoh asked for incense to be burned so people would remain calm and asked that the story of what was seen be written down.

The Search for Extra Terrestial Intelligence, the SETI project, began in America in 1959. NASA helped from 1988 to 1991. Two of the people who have put money into the search since have been Steven Spielberg and Arthur C. Clarke.

The term UFO is said to have come from the 1956 book by US Air Force captain Edward Ruppelt, The *Report on Unidentified Flying Objects*.

 Astronauts going to the Moon in 1969 were given an ET Law. By this law they were to force any person they thought had come into contact with aliens to go into NASA quarantine.

The first known photo of a UFO was taken by astronomer Jose Bonilla through a telescope at Zacatecas, Mexico, in August 1883.

The weather can play tricks that are mistaken for UFOs, visions and strange lights. Clouds can form into disc shapes. A group of these 'flying saucer' clouds was photographed over Santos, Brazil. They look just like UFOs from a distance. In cold air ice crystals can pile into columns which reflect sunlight. When a snow cloud crosses the column, it looks as if a giant cross, which is lit up by the sun, appears in the sky.

What you should do if you see a UFO . . .

1. Keep calm.
2. Note down the time you see the object.
3. Try and work out how high it is in the sky.
4. Note where it is going – towards you, away from you, from left to right or right to left or in all sorts of ways.
5. Try and guess the speed.
6. Remember the colour. Does the colour change?
7. Tell someone what you have seen soon afterwards.
8. If you cannot tell someone soon, try and write down what you observed.
9. If you can, take a photo with your mobile phone.

Gruesome Ghosts

John Buckstone loved the Haymarket Theatre in London. Though he died in 1878 his ghost turns up in the dressing rooms of the theatre from time to time. He is said to only appear when things are going well.

It is believed that no ghost can cross a flowing stream.

The ghost of a Second World War Wellington bomber has been seen flying down the Towy valley in Wales. It was completely silent.

Many people believe that they have lived previous lives. This is more common in Asia, where reincarnation is accepted. General Patton, the US general of the Second World War, believed he had been a Roman warrior.

A number of people have been said to be able to predict the future. Some have been very close to what actually happened: Robert Nixon, called the 'Cheshire Idiot', foretold the English Civil War and the Great Fire of London over 100 years before they happened.

Nostradamus, the famous French seer who died in 1566, wrote a book of his predictions, often known as Centuries. In the book he predicted the rise of Napoleon, the success of Louis Pasteur (the French chemist), the arrival of a dictator in Germany (except he called him Hister instead of Hitler), and the abdication of King Edward VIII of Britain.

David Croly, an American who died in 1889, predicted the First World War, the arrival of cinema, multinational companies and air travel.

Count Hamon, a British clairvoyant, predicted the sinking of the *Titanic* and the death of the First World War British leader Lord Kitchener. In 1904, he very accurately predicted the murder of Rasputin in Russia. His other predictions included the Boer War, the First World War and a separate India and Pakistan.

There are said to be more ghosts per square mile in Britain than in any other country.

Many people claim to have seen the phantom funeral train of President Lincoln of the USA, which is said to retrace the route of the original train of 1865 every year on the anniversary of President Lincoln's funeral.

Often a Ouija board is used in seances – meetings which are said to conjure up spirits of the departed. The board was invented early in the century and called after the French and German words for 'Yes' (*Oui* and *Ja*).

The ghost of Anne Boleyn, the wife of Henry VIII, is said to return to Blickling Hall, Norfolk, each year on 19 May, the day she was executed in 1536. She sits in a coach pulled by four headless horses and driven by a headless coachman. She carries her own head on her knees. The coach drives up to the house and then disappears when it reaches the front door.

Strange weather and falls from the sky have been recorded for centuries:

1. In 1847 a 50 kg block of ice fell over Ayrshire, Scotland. At the time there were no balloons, aeroplanes or other flying machines from which a block of ice could have fallen. Where the block of ice came from remains a mystery.

2. During the Second World War there was a shower of frogs over Alton Towers, the big house in Staffordshire, for an hour and a half.

3. On a bright June day in 1948, Ian Pate, at Barton on Sea, near Bournemouth, saw fish falling from

the sky. They covered 100 metres. There was not a cloud in the sky.

4. A shower of hazelnuts fell from a clear blue sky in March near Westbury Park in Bristol in March 1977.
5. Insect eggs in jelly fell from the sky at Eton, Berkshire, in midsummer, 1911.
6. Rain fell from a clear sky at Grayshott, Hampshire, in 1929, 1931 and 1933.
7. Frogs fell from the sky near Whittington military barracks, Staffordshire, in September 1956.
8. It rained pennies and halfpennies at Hanham in Avon in September 1956.
9. Eggs fell from the sky at Wokingham in Berkshire in December 1974.
10. In July 1888 rain was reported falling from a clear sky at Stevenage in Hertfordshire.

While there have been ghost trains, a ghost lift is unusual! When the Palace Hotel in Southport on Merseyside was being demolished in 1969, the lift took on a life of its own. Even when all the power was off, the lift moved – its doors opened and closed, its lights flashed and it went up and down. What was even odder was that the brake for the lift was on – so it shouldn't have moved at all!

The ghost of Catherine Howard, one of the wives of Henry VIII, is heard as shrieks in the haunted gallery of Hampton Court Palace; she is heard running along the gallery and into the chapel at the end. She was beheaded on February 13 1542.

A monster was seen on a lake at the edge of a forest in Java in 1975. It was said to be a six-metre-long prehistoric monster. It looked like a giant fish or turtle. Local fishermen burned opium on the lake to keep the monster happy.

King Charles I arrived at Northampton in 1645, prepared to do battle with Oliver Cromwell's army the next day. He stayed at the Wheatsheaf hotel in the town. During the night he was visited by the ghost of Lord Stafford, his friend and adviser, who had been killed early in the Civil War. The ghost twice told Charles he should leave Northampton and take his army north. The king decided to do what the ghost told him, frightened by what might happen if he did not take the advice. However, Charles's generals persuaded him to stay and the battle was fought at Naseby on June 14. In the battle the King's forces suffered a heavy defeat. The Cavaliers never recovered from this battle and Charles ended up losing everything, finally being executed in London.

The only British Prime Minister to be assassinated was Spencer Perceval. He dreamed of the event on May 10 1812. The next morning he told his dream to his family and friends. They tried to persuade him not to go to the House of Commons that day, but he went all the same. Things turned out as he had seen in his dream.

Four kings and queens are said to haunt Windsor Castle, including Elizabeth I.

Poltergeists are said to be spirits which are able to move things and make noises. They are mostly harmless. A poltergeist was found in a Welsh farmhouse in 1904. It threw all sorts of things around, moved pictures, dropped crockery, mixed up food and wrote little messages all over the house. One night ten people, including a policeman, sat up to watch for this spirit. After a time it arrived. The first thing it did was pick up a lump of butter and throw it into the face of the policeman!

One night during the First World War in 1915, a young Adolf Hitler was serving in the German Army in the trenches. At dinner time, he was sitting down when he heard a voice which told him to move twenty metres. He did so. As soon as he sat down again, a shell hit the part of the trench he had just left. Everyone was killed. Hitler took the strange warning to be a great omen for his future.

 The Swedish writer Swedenborg arrived at the port of Gothenburg in Sweden in September 1759. He went to have dinner with an English friend in the town. During the meal he suddenly turned very pale and announced that fire was sweeping through the Swedish capital Stockholm – 480 km away. Upset by his vision he left the house, coming back only a short time later to say that the fire was now under control and had stopped only three doors from his own home. The next evening a courier was able to confirm that everything had happened as Swedenborg had described!

In Somerset, toast is dipped in cider and hung on apple trees to drive off evil spirits.

On a clear December day a ship, the *Dei Gratia*, was sailing across the Atlantic when another vessel, with two sails set, was sighted in the distance. As the *Dei Gratia* moved closer, no one could be seen on the deck of the other ship. Three men were sent over to examine the seemingly deserted vessel. As they approached the desolate ship, they found it was the *Mary Celeste*, which had sailed out of New

York. As they clambered aboard, the three called out for anyone – there was no reply. The ship's boat was missing. They searched the ship and there was no one on board, though the captain's bed was unmade, the pots and pans in the galley were all in place, and everything else seemed in order. The only strange thing was a dampness throughout the ship. Reaching the cargo of alcohol, they found it all in place. The crew of the *Dei Gratia* were mystified by the state of the ship. A skeleton crew was ordered to take the ship in hand and sail it to the Azores. What happened to the *Mary Celeste* remains a mystery. It was obvious that all aboard had taken to the boat, but no trace of them was ever found.

A prison doctor, Ernest Helby, was riding his motorbike on a road across Dartmoor, the desolate moorland in Devon, in 1921. In his sidecar he carried his two children. Suddenly he told them to jump out. The motorbike swerved off the road and the doctor was killed in the crash. The children survived and later said they had seen a pair of ghostly hairy hands on the handlebars just before the crash. About eight weeks later, a young army officer was thrown from his motorbike on the same road. Afterwards he explained that he had seen a pair of hairy hands appear over his own and he lost control of the bike. The hands are said to be those of an Italian who worked at a nearby gunpowder factory. One day, after drinking, he went into the factory and forgot to take off his boots. The boots had nails in their soles and made a spark. The explosion blew the man to bits.

A red ghost appeared to Henry IV of France in 1610, predicting his death the next day. The same ghost was seen by the bed of the French Emperor Napoleon by his doctor on 5 May 1821, just before Napoleon died.

Throughout 1996, there were many protestors at the place where a new road, the Newbury by-pass, was to be built in southern England. The planned route would cause the destruction of woodland and that meant many animals would lose their homes. By the end of the summer the last of the protestors had left and the security guards thought they would be left in peace. However, in December, some of the guards became very frightened by the unexpected. They saw the ghosts of Roundhead and Cavalier soldiers who had fought the battle of Newbury on that spot during the Civil War over three hundred and fifty years before!

People in a house in West Yorkshire were terrified by a pair of gloves. The gloves appeared at the bottom and top of the doors, like a gruesome pair of hands! When an aunt in the room began to sing a hymn to get rid of the spirit, the gloves began to tap out the time of the hymn.

The writer C. S. Lewis, famous for *The Chronicles of Narnia*, had many friends and many people he wrote to. A few days after he died in 1963 one of the friends was sitting watching television one evening when C. S. Lewis suddenly appeared, sitting in a chair close by, and spoke to the friend. The apparition had a redder face than normal, but otherwise looked quite well. Having said a few words which helped the friend with a problem, he disappeared. A week later, while the friend was reading in bed, just before going to sleep, Lewis appeared again, repeating the words of a few days before. And again, he disappeared.

There are several ghosts at the Houses of Parliament. A woman in pink has been seen at the west front of the House of Lords, where the Palace of Westminster used to be. Another of the ghosts is a man in black seen wandering the galleries from time to time.

The ghost of the first wife of the British poet Shelley, who died about 150 years ago, has been seen in Hyde Park, London. She drowned herself in the lake in the park, the Serpentine.

The Loch Ness monster was first sighted in about AD 565 when St Columba is said to have driven the monster away from a swimmer in the loch.

During the plague in London in 1665, flaming swords, coffins, ghosts and angels were seen over the city.

A haunted house in the north of Britain once had a ghost who appeared when his relatives put his photo away. He only disappeared after his photo was put back on display.

A ghost is said to haunt the Drury Lane Theatre, London. It is the figure of a young man who was murdered there in 1780. To see him is said to bring success. The skeleton of the man was found by workmen early in the last century, entombed in a wall. There were still the shreds of a grey riding coat covering the skeleton, and a dagger was sticking out of the ribs.

In a broken-down house in Hydesville, New York state, America, there lived a poor Canadian, John D. Fox. He had three children. One March morning in 1848, the children heard knocks and raps in the house. The noises went on for days, until the noise and movement was so strong that the old house shook. One of the girls, Catherine, aged 7, clapped to answer the knocks. Almost at once a clap answered. Next she snapped her fingers. Again, the sound came back. Her sister Margaret, aged 10, joined in and again there was an answer. Margaret went to get her parents and showed them what happened. The amazed mother and father began to work out a way to 'talk' to the ghost by knocks – and it answered! The spirit said it was the ghost of Charles Rosma, a peddler who had been murdered there. The story of the haunted house became so well known in America that the two sisters toured the country.

The ghost of Abraham Lincoln, the president of the United States who was assassinated by John Wilkes Booth in 1865, haunts the White House in Washington. About 60 years ago a maid saw his ghost sitting on the edge of a bed, taking off his shoes. In 1945 Lincoln's ghost was seen by the Dutch queen Wilhelmina, while she was staying at the White House.

On 4 August 1951, two English sisters-in-law were staying at Puys, a seaside village near Dieppe on the north French coast. They were awoken in the very early morning by men shouting. These sounds were followed by the sound of gunfire and aeroplanes at about four in the morning. They looked out, but could see nothing. They could not explain what happened. The noises of battle continued for almost three hours, until there was silence at about seven in the morning. It is thought that the women had heard a ghost battle. It was the battle that took place at Dieppe some seven years before.

It is not what you expect at work. The ghost of the 4th Duke of Norfolk used to wander about Coutts Bank in London. He'd been beheaded for treason in 1512. Receptionists saw the headless ghost wandering about, dressed in Elizabethan clothes.

The most common feeling when ghosts appear is that the air goes very chilly.

Sir Arthur Conan Doyle, the creator of Sherlock Holmes, spent many years investigating ghosts and the unexplained.

Margaret Sheridan came across a ghost when she was about 17 at her family house in Frampton, England. At the time her father was in France, fighting in the First World War. Margaret was coming down the stairs for tea one day when she saw a boy on the stairs. He wore a white sailor suit and a straw hat on his head. He was about her age. The two looked at each other, but did not speak as they passed each other. Margaret thought the stranger was a guest. She went in to tea and told everyone there she had seen the boy in the sailor's costume on the stairs. No one spoke. Later, Margaret found out that the boy was the ghost of an ancestor who had died at sea. He would appear in the house when the heir to the Sheridan family was about to die. A few days later a letter arrived saying that Margaret's father had been killed in the war.

The Society for Psychical Research is a group which looks into stories of ghosts and other strange things. It was formed over 100 years ago.

On a walk in Austria, the writer Barbara Cartland and her brother came across a fairy-tale castle. When they told villagers about this marvellous building, they were astonished to be told that the castle had been destroyed years before.

When Mrs Lincoln, the wife of President Lincoln, had her photo taken after the President had died, the photograph included a ghostly image of the President.

At least four skulls which are said to scream if anyone tries to bury them are kept in Britain.

At Beverley in Yorkshire a video was taken of the rooms in an empty house. When the film was played back, the image of a girl appeared. She was believed to be the ghost of a maid who had killed herself in the house.

On a winter's night, after a long day at work, Dr Mitchell of Philadelphia in the USA heard his doorbell ring. Opening the door, he saw a small girl. She said her mother was very sick and could he come at once. She would show him the way. The doctor followed the girl. He found the woman very ill and at once gave her medicine to help her get better. As he was leaving the room, the doctor remarked that the woman was lucky to have such a helpful daughter. The woman was very surprised. She told the doctor that her daughter had died about a month before!

Vile Vampires

 In the first stories about vampires, told over 2,000 years ago, the vampire was said to have been a dragon who ate the moon. The legend came to Europe from the Far East and stories began to be told of vampires who sucked the blood of babies and people.

 From very early on, vampires, ghosts, werewolves and spirits were known as the 'undead'. Only in the 1400s were the different types of the 'undead' defined.

 During October 1989 it was reported that vampire bats had killed seven people in the Amazon jungle in Peru. The people died because the bats passed rabies on to them.

 When a werewolf dies, it is believed to become a vampire. This is why stories of vampires and werewolves are closely connected. In the Slovenian language the word for vampire is *vukodlak*, which means 'wolf's hair'.

 The Chinese vampire is said to live by the light of the moon.

It is said that the writer Bram Stoker came up with the idea of *Dracula* after a nightmare he had following a dinner of crabs.

 The word vampire comes from the Hungarian word *vampir*.

 The original Dracula was a nasty man known as Vlad the Impaler, a murderous medieval tyrant who lived in Wallachia, Romania. He was also known as *Draculaea*, the son of the Devil. He often killed off his enemies by having them stuck on very sharp pointed poles which formed a horrific avenue up to the walls of his castle. There is no record of the original Dracula actually drinking blood.

 It is said that once a person is bitten by a vampire he or she dies and then returns as a pale vampire – one of the legion of the 'undead'.

 During medieval times, Dracula was thought to have a body and soul. His body ate things like roast beef, as well as drinking blood. His soul ate meringues and fruit in whipped cream!

In the 19th century people in the Ukraine and Russia thought that vampires were dead wizards, witches or werewolves.

Whatever you do, don't annoy your mum or dad. In medieval Europe, anyone cursed by their parents was said to become a vampire when they died.

In Romania, if you are the seventh son in a family, you are said to be more likely to become a vampire.

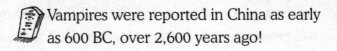

Vampires were reported in China as early as 600 BC, over 2,600 years ago!

In Romania, fir trees are planted over graves. These trees are said to keep away vampires.

A vampire can see in the dark. Sometimes their eyes will turn blood-red so they can see better when there is no light.

It is said that you can stop a vampire from moving by putting a branch of a wild rose in his coffin – he won't dare move in case he pricks his rotten skin.

In Eastern Europe vampires are said to have two hearts and two souls, so that when one dies the other remains undead.

Romanian legend says that vampires meet up in places where no dog can be heard barking and no cuckoo sings.

Vampires can apparently enter into locked houses through chimneys or keyholes. They won't come in if you put garlic by the chimney or rub it on the keyholes.

 A vampire bat can fly, walk and turn somersaults. Vampire bats suck blood through tubes made by their tongues and lower lips. In a laboratory they will crowd round a dish of blood and lick it up. Any vampire bat imported to Britain is liable to be kept in a cage away from other animals, in quarantine, for life. A vampire bat can only drink about three millilitres of blood a day. It would take weeks to kill someone at that rate.

 In the 1400s doctors told nobles in Europe that they would feel much better if they drank the blood of their subjects!

The legends of vampires and demons are very old. Many people believe they don't exist at all, yet something very odd was found in a burial mound at Sayre in Pennsylvania in the 1880s. It was the skull of a two-metre-tall person, with horns! Most surprising was that the burial took place about AD 1200. Some of the bones were sent to a museum in Philadelphia but the mystery will probably never be solved as the bones have since disappeared!

Bram Stoker got his inspiration for Dracula's pointy teeth from English explorer and writer Sir Richard Burton.

 The vampire of Malaya has the strange name Penanggalan and is female. She is supposed to be a monster who sucks the blood of children. She comes into houses where children live by forcing her way through the floor.

 A German and Dutch legend states that a vampire can be destroyed by cutting off its head with a spade. The spade has to be new. The severed head then has to be carried to the nearest stream and thrown in.

 In 1732 a vampire was reported in Belgrade, the capital of Serbia. The creature was seen leaning to one side and had long, crooked fingernails. Around its mouth were drops of blood.

 In Portugal there is a legend about a vampire bird-woman, called the Bruxsa, who is said to suck the blood of children.

 For hundreds of years animals were kept away from graves because it was believed that if a bird flew over a dead body, or a cat jumped on the grave, then the body would turn into a vampire.

Many people believed that the bubonic plague, which swept through Europe at various times and killed millions, was caused by vampires.

 You can keep a vampire away by showing them a crucifix or the shape of a cross. If you prefer, you can keep them away all the time by wearing a necklace of smelly garlic!

 Some creatures begin to behave like vampires. Finches on Wolf Island, one of the Galápagos Islands, have learned to drink the blood of living animals.

Seven ways to beat a vampire:
1. Sprinkle chalk and holy water nearby.
2. Cut off its head with a spade.
3. Stick a wooden or iron stake through its heart.
4. Pour boiling water down a hole near its grave.
5. Reflect sunlight into the tomb of the vampire. It will burn up.
6. Fill the mouth of the vampire with garlic.
7. Hold a crucifix or cross up to the vampire.

 Legends of evil spirits who suck blood are ancient and exist all over the world. In the Nicobar Islands there are sculptures of people with teeth the size of tusks.

In Serbia it was believed that a vampire could open locked chests, levitate logs of burning wood from fires and turn cattle crazy.

 In Greece, for a time, blue eyes were thought to be the mark of a vampire.

 In 1951, Dr Herbert Mayo of America concluded that vampires were really people who had been buried alive.

 In many countries the vampire can take on the shape of other animals – like bats or wolves – and has the power to control the creatures of the night.

 During the 16th century, detailed stories of vampires were written by clerks. In one case a vampire who had been buried for five years was said to have risen up and killed his brother and nieces. He was said to be able to survive for a fortnight from a feast of blood. When his grave was opened, it was said his heart was still beating. An iron bar was driven through his chest and his head was cut off.

In the ancient Middle East, babies were given small carved wood tablets to wear round their necks in order to ward off a female demon that wanted to suck their blood.

 Female vampire Countess Bathory of Hungary had baths in her victims' blood. When she was found out she was sentenced to be walled up alive in the castle where she lived! A small slit was made in the wall so she could be fed. She died after four years.

 During the Middle Ages some people in Europe had a rare disease which made them bleed. The condition meant that they had to keep out of sunlight. This strange behaviour led to stories of people drinking blood at night – adding to the vampire legend.

 The first British vampires, known as the 'bloodsucking corpses', were described by William of Newburgh. He was a monk who mentioned these monsters in two books written over 800 years ago.

Over 30,000 people were said to have been werewolves in Europe between 1520 and 1650!

Fears of evil spirits, not just vampires, lasted well into the 19th century in Britain. Prime Minister Benjamin Disraeli left the legs of his bed in bowls of salt water to ward off evil spirits.

In German stories the vampire casts no shadow.

Some people believe that a vampire can turn into fog or a pile of straw.

Romanian stories suggest that vampires have short tails which grow thicker when it gets warm.

The vampire hunter in Bram Stoker's *Dracula* was Professor Van Helsing. Van Helsing always carried with him a pair of pincers, a mallet and a stake in a medical bag. This was his 'getting rid of vampires' kit.

Just to be sure that a vampire was properly destroyed, the Romanians would carry out one of the three following safety measures:

1. Drive a nail into the forehead of the vampire.
2. Pierce the body of the vampire with needles.
3. Smear the corpse with pig fat.

When the plague hit a part of Austria in 1710, vampires were blamed. All the tombs in one local cemetery were opened up to try and catch the vampires!

In medieval times it was said that the dead bled from their wounds if they were near the person (or people) who had murdered them. Shakespeare liked this idea and used it in his famous play *Richard III*.

James I of England and VI of Scotland was a fan of vampires. He wrote about them in a pamphlet titled *Demonology* in 1597.

In Saxony, Germany, a lemon was put in the mouth of a vampire to make sure it did not come back. Just to be doubly sure it didn't move, the corpse was then nailed into the coffin.

The fear of being mistaken for dead was so great in the 1800s that over 200 books were written about avoiding being buried alive.

Vampires are said to have bodies that do not decay. They are kept in perfect condition by drinking blood. There are many real bodies which reportedly have not decayed after death. Among them is that of Saint Bobola of Russia. His body was found intact 72 years after he was murdered.

 To protect against vampire attack, a tar cross was put on the doors and windows of houses in Serbia.

In Elizabethan times the equivalent of aspirin was powdered human skull dissolved in red wine!

 American Vincent Hillyer was allowed to stay in Dracula's castle for one night in 1977. Afterwards he described being woken by the smell of flowers. There were no flowers on the rock on which the castle was built and certainly no flowers in the ruins! Following his night in the famous castle Vincent was taken to hospital as he complained of feeling faint. In the clinic he was found to have puncture wounds on his neck! The doctor said they were only the bites of a large spider. But were they?

The idea of levitation became popular in Victorian times. From the 1850s a man called Daniel Home was seen to levitate his body. Through 40 years of demonstrations no one could prove he was faking.

In 1304 it was reported that one body was buried five times. Each time it turned up not far from the grave and had to be reburied.

The stake used to destroy a vampire can be made from aspen or hawthorn – aspen because it was the wood of Christ's Cross and hawthorn because it was the base for the Crown of Thorns.

In Romania it is said that a stake has to be used on a vampire at first light. In order for it to be effective it has to strike the heart on the first attempt.

In the 18th century, people who learned medicine were sometimes accused of creating vampires! It was common for bodies which were to be used for anatomy to be left in the open during cold winters to preserve them. People who did not know this thought the bodies were vampires and ordered them to be burned.

Legend has it that if you catch a vampire and you don't have a stake, you should cut off its head. You should then throw the head into a stream or pond. The head will either sink through the earth, to be burned up on the inside of the world, or be carried out to sea and then drop down to be burned up below the Earth's crust.

 Among the best-known bloodsuckers are leeches. They are still used in medicine today. A large leech can drink or suck in 30 grams of blood at one go.

Some of the ancient Romans behaved like vampires. Fresh gladiator blood was drunk in Rome as a cure for epilepsy.

Beastly Bodies

 Captain Cook and his crew were the first British explorers to see tattoos. They saw them on the natives of the Pacific island of Tahiti, when they landed there in 1769.

 Victims of disasters can become diabetic for a short time – about ten days – as a result of shock.

 In the twelfth century Henry 1 of England decreed that a yard was equal to the distance from the end of his nose to the end of his thumb when his arm was stretched out.

 There is enough of the chemical phosphorus in a normal human body to make 2,200 matches!

 A baby can get hiccups before it is born.

 From 13 June 1948 until 1 June 1949 a person in Los Angeles hiccuped 160 million times. People sent in 60,000 suggestions for cures. Vera Stone, aged 18, hiccuped for 59 days in 1929. Nothing she tried seemed to stop the attack. Her doctor thought she might have forgotten how to stop and decided to make her think of something else. He gave her

a drug which made her feel ill but also put her to sleep. When Vera woke up she forgot to hiccup because she was paying attention to her other sickness. It did not take long for her to get better.

 Edwin Robinson was in a road crash which left him blind and almost unable to hear. His doctors said he would not get better. In June 1980, going out to check on his pet chicken at his home in America, he was struck by lightning and knocked out. He came to twenty minutes later and found he could see and hear. A month later he also found hair beginning to grow again on his bald head!

 There are 2 square metres of skin on each fully grown body.

 The bodies of Australian aborigines cannot deal with air conditioning. If they stay in a place with air conditioning they lose body heat and can die of cold.

In north-west China in 1995, a dentist completed a three-metre tower from teeth he had taken out. He built it to frighten villagers into looking after their teeth.

Babies can be born naturally or can be born by Caesarean section, when a cut is made in the mother to let the baby out. The name came from the son of the ancient Roman Emperor Julius Caesar, who is said to have been born in this way. This method of being born was not used in Europe again for hundreds of years. The first time it was re-used was in 1500 in Switzerland – the operation was carried out by a butcher! The first Caesarean operation in Britain took place in a hospital in Blackburn, Lancashire, in 1793.

Caroline Clare of Canada is reported to have been magnetic. Knives and forks could be attached to her skin and stay there without any obvious help.

The first great outbreak of the bubonic plague, known as the Black Death, happened in Britain in June 1348, at Melcombe, Weymouth, in Dorset. By the time the plague was over, up to a quarter of the people in Europe had died.

The Pedaung women of Burma stretch their necks with large numbers of brass rings.

During a terrific thunder and lightning storm in Arizona, USA, in 1929, the lightning lit up the eerie outline of a dark horseman, sitting absolutely still in his saddle out on the open plain. Once the storm had passed, a search party was sent out to find rancher Roy Sorrell. They found him – the man and his horse were standing stock-still on the plain. Both man and horse had been struck by a lightning bolt and killed; they remained 'frozen' just as they had been when the lightning struck.

 Many people who are left-handed play golf, cricket and other games right-handed.

The tongue is the strongest muscle in the body. It is the only muscle which is attached at only one end.

 Diabetes is a disease in which people are unable to make insulin. It was first identified in Germany in 1889. It was found that the body makes insulin to control the amount of sugar in the body. Up to 1923 most of those who had diabetes died early. That year three doctors in Canada, Banting, Best and MacLeod, were able to produce insulin. This made it possible for diabetics to live a near-normal life with injections.

About 1771, Edward Jenner, an English student doctor, met a milkmaid in the country. She told him that she could not catch the disease smallpox because she had already had a mild form of the disease, cowpox, which she had caught from the cows she milked. Jenner decided this example might be repeated. He started to deliberately infect people with a mild form of a disease to prevent them catching a more serious infection. After experiments he found this idea of 'vaccination' worked. By 1801 over 100,000 people had been vaccinated against smallpox in Britain. This success led to the use of vaccination across the world.

 Lady Montagu (1690–1762) introduced inoculation against smallpox into England. Centuries before, when King Edward I of England fell ill with smallpox, his doctor covered his entire body with a scarlet cloth. The king was cured.

> The first kidney transplant, which took place in America in 1954, involved identical twins.

 Percy Oliver organized the first blood transfusion service in the world in London in 1921. The first blood transfusions ever used animal blood.

Professor Christiaan Barnard of South Africa decided to try a heart transplant on a person in late 1967. In December he transplanted a girl's heart into the body of Louis Washkansky. Though his patient lived only eighteen days after the operation, Professor Barnard had proved a human heart transplant was possible.

A man in Wisconsin, USA, hibernated each winter for twenty-three years from November to Easter.

The strength of some people is extraordinary. An 18th-century strongman, Thomas Topham, could click his fingers while a man danced on each of his outstretched arms!

Blood takes one minute to be pumped round the body and return to the heart.

A French monk who died in 1609 aged 70 only ate one meal a day for 48 years. It consisted of bread, water and a few raw roots.

By the time a person is 50, their nails will have grown a total of 2 metres.

The big toe has only two bones, the other toes three. Webbed toes and fingers are quite common. The second and third toes often have extra skin which makes them webbed, usually on both feet.

 An adult human heart beats 60 to 70 times a minute. The heart of a baby beats about 130 times a minute. By the age of three the heart has slowed to 100 beats a minute, then down to about 90 a minute by the age of 12.

 Some people have a disease which means they cannot cry. The South African leader Nelson Mandela is one person who cannot cry. His many years in prison, where he broke rocks, stopped his eyes from making tears.

 Teeth do not stay still. They move in the mouth for most of a person's life. Tooth decay is the world's most common disease.

 Some well-known people ended up being buried in strange places. Both Emperor Selassie of Ethiopia, a hero to Rastafarians, and the great Indian poet Sheik Zauq, were buried under lavatories.

 Dutch giant Jan Van Albert was 2.87 metres tall in 1920.

 Siamese twins are called after Chang and Eng Bunker, who were born joined together in

Siam (Thailand) in 1811. They were put on
show in Europe and America. They lived to
the age of 62. They married two sisters and
had 22 children. They died within an hour of
each other.

 Teeth are the only bits of a person which do not
grow back. Charles Land of Detroit, USA, was the
man who invented porcelain caps for broken teeth.

 The average person swallows 295 times while eating
a meal. Until they are seven months old, babies can
swallow and breathe at the same time.

 A human can survive for about five weeks without
food, about five days without water, but only for about
five minutes without air. There are some extraordinary
exceptions – Brian Cunningham of Jackson, Michigan
in the USA, was revived after he had spent 38 minutes
trapped underwater!

The heart in almost all humans is on the left side.
When it turns up on the right, all the other internal
bits are also moved from left to right. Some people
can be very different. During World War One, an
Australian soldier went to hospital for some trouble
with a leg. He was found to have two hearts! They
beat one after the other.

Forty per cent of people in space suffer from space sickness.

 The skin on the bottom of your feet is thicker than at any other place on your body. The average pair of feet will sweat about half a pint of perspiration a day. During a normal day a person will take about 18,000 steps. In an average lifetime, a person will walk the equivalent of almost three times round the world.

 If calcium is taken out of human bones, they become so rubbery that they can be tied in a knot like rope or string.

 The Russian Siamese twins Irina and Galiana had one torso, two arms, four legs and two heads. They were very different. One was calm, the other excitable. They had one nervous system and slept at different times. They were proof that sleep is controlled by the brain.

 One person in twenty has an extra rib.

 Eskimos have extra flaps on their noses so they are not frozen when it is very cold.

 Most babies who are born premature are left-handed.

 There are up to 8 million hairs on a normal body.

The King of Siam (now Thailand) who came to the throne in 1851 had 82 children by 32 wives.

 A woman's tears are one of the strongest natural antiseptics.

 The tallest woman whose height has been proven was Jane Bunford. She was born in England in 1895. She was 7 foot 7 inches tall. If she did not have a curved spine, she would have been 7 foot 11 inches tall. Her hair also broke records – it was 8 foot long. How often she washed it is not recorded. She died at the age of 27 in 1922.

Humans cry from the time they are born until they die. It is a slow tear that cleans the eyeballs and stops them drying out. When we blink this water is spread to protect the eyes. On average we blink 25 times a minute.

Three quarters of human blood is water. We can lose 3 pints of blood without harm. An average adult has between 9 and 12 pints of blood.

 Twins are often ill at the same time, even if they are miles apart. In September 1996 twins Barbara Gamblin and Sue Sycamore, aged 45, were taken to the same hospital at the same time on the same day after separate accidents. Twins' teeth also decay or fall out at much the same time.

 The tallest people in the world are the men of the Watutsi tribe of central Africa; they grow up to 2.3 metres tall.

 The human stomach can deal with many unusual things being eaten without the person being sick. Some people have set records for eating strange things. The most extreme case is that of Frenchman Michel Lotito. He ate the whole of a Cessna light aircraft, finishing on Boxing Day 1996.

 The heart of a dead person was made to beat again for the first time by a Russian doctor in 1946.

 Chinese or Asian people have up to 30,000 more hairs on their heads than white people with red hair. A natural blonde has about 20,000 more hairs on his or her head than an Asian.

 Scotland has the highest proportion of red-headed people in the world. Eleven per cent of the population has red hair.

 Everyone has dandruff. No one yet knows why it happens.

The electricity in an average human body could keep a lightbulb alight for three minutes.

 Sixty per cent of a human body is water – about 10 gallons altogether. The water is about one sixth of a person's weight.

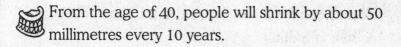 During the night a human body grows by about a centimetre. It goes back to normal size during the day.

From the age of 40, people will shrink by about 50 millimetres every 10 years.

A mother in Sydney, Australia, gave birth to twins 56 days apart and in two different years. The first twin was born on 16 December 1952 and the other on 10 February 1953.

In 1994 a Mr A. Z. Hamock was buried in Kentucky, USA. He had died in 1948. He had been preserved by his family with a home-made embalming fluid, dressed in his evening clothes, and put on a seat in the family home.

 If skin is transplanted from one person to another it shrinks and dies. The only time this does not happen is if the two people are identical twins.

125

It is impossible to sneeze and keep your eyes open at the same time.

 A human bite is more dangerous than that of a dog, a cat or a horse.

It is said tombstones were first put over graves to stop the dead becoming zombies and harming the living.

In adults, hair will grow for about three years, then rest for three months. At this time any loose hair falls out.

In an average life a person will eat 50 tonnes of food and drink 50,000 litres of liquid.

 Bodies can be preserved by embalming or by freezing. Freezing the body is called cryogenics. Among famous people whose bodies have been kept are Lenin and the former head of the Philippines, Ferdinand Marcos. Marcos's body is kept in a fridge. He was put in an airtight glass casket, clutching a rosary and with made-up face and hands. Chemicals will keep his remains fresh for years. When the coffin of King Charles I of England, who had been beheaded, was opened two hundred years after he died, it was found that his hair, beard, face and blue eyes were preserved. One of the people present took a bit of his hair and one of his bones as souvenirs. King Charles I was not very tall: even when he had his head, he was only 1.40 metres.

 The second hand on a watch was invented by a doctor, Sir John Floyer, about 300 years ago, so doctors could check a person's heartbeat.

 The first American President, George Washington, had three sets of false teeth – one of wood, one of iron and one of ivory. He found the ivory false teeth useless for chewing, but they did taste nice – he kept them in a glass of port every night to improve their flavour.

 There are over 600 muscles in the body. They are all used for different actions. At least twelve muscles are needed to pick up a pencil, seventeen to smile and 200 pairs to walk.

The great English painter Constable, famous for the Hay Wain, is believed to have had colour blindness. He was, it seems, unable to see red and green clearly. Because of this the greens and reds in his pictures of the countryside are very bright. Colour blindness is passed on to children by their mother.

Richard III of England, Louis XIV of France and the Emperor Napoleon of France were all born with teeth.

 The Danish astronomer Tycho Brahe, who died in 1601, had a gold false nose. He lost his real nose in a sword fight.

 Eyelashes do not turn white as we get older. Each eyelash lasts about 5 months.

 One in ten people is left-handed. Prince William is left-handed. His great-grandfather, King George VI, was born left-handed but was taught to write with his right hand. No one knows why, but left-handed people die younger than right-handed people. Other famous left-handed people include the artists Picasso and Michelangelo and the early film star Charles Chaplin. When typing, the left hand does fifty-six per cent of the work. Oddly, the number of left-handed men is double the number of left-handed women.

Mad Medicine

In February 1931, *Life* magazine in the USA reported that a doctor in Joliet, Illinois, had called a Chicago specialist by phone to ask about a small blood transfusion for a child. The specialist said to use the parent's blood for the operation. The doctor thought he said 'parrot's blood'. A search was undertaken to find a parrot whose owner would give permission for some blood to be extracted. About 1.5 teaspoonfuls of parrot blood were transferred to the infant, who had been suffering from paralysis. The infant immediately improved and the parrot recovered fully after coming round from the ether.

Among the first drains built for public health were those in India about 5,000 years ago.

In 1346 lepers were forbidden to live in large towns or cities in Britain. The punishment for those who let them into their homes was confiscation of their property.

Bethlehem Hospital, London, became an institution for the insane in 1407. It gave rise to the word 'Bedlam' for a madhouse.

Gold was first used for filling teeth in about 1450. During the Middle Ages fillings were made of wax or gum.

 In England, barbers gave the first lessons in dentistry in about 1460.

 The incubator for babies born early was invented in Paris in about 1900 and first used in the Paris Maternity Hospital. It had been designed by a Dr Tarnier and was based on one built for the director of the Paris zoo, for premature lions!

Sir John Hawkins, the Tudor sailor and adventurer, was among the first to tackle the disease scurvy, which caused swelling in the limbs, bleeding under the skin, weakness and body pains, as a result of a lack of vitamins. He cured a whole ship's company by giving them lemon juice to drink. The idea of using lime juice was only widely used in the 18th century when Sir George Blane suggested the Navy use it. The Royal Navy made it compulsory on board ships in 1795.

 A dentist, Dr John Long, of Daytona Beach, Florida, confirmed that one of his patients, a housewife, was able to pick up radio stations through her metal fillings. He said the effect would last only a few days. Close to the time when the effect was due to wear off the woman held a party for her friends. When she opened her mouth to laugh, out came the sound of the theme tune from the film *Dr Zhivago*, followed by 'Rambling Rose'. Some of her friends danced to the music.

One of the most awe-inspiring British inventions used in surgery is the Q-switch. This little gadget turns a harmless 60-watt ray of light, no stronger than the light from a lightbulb, into a laser beam of 60 kilowatts – strong enough to vaporize 'everything it touches'. It is used for delicate eye surgery – but also to cut diamonds and engrave computer chips!

During the 19th century many people in Germany fell ill with a mystery sickness and a number died. A doctor noticed that the disease only happened in houses with green wallpaper. On examination it was found that the green colour contained enough of the deadly poison arsenic to kill 900 people.

 About 500 new human illnesses are discovered each year.

The world's first dentists were thought to be the Incas, until in 1997, a skull was found of an Anglo-Saxon, complete with an iron false tooth. The warrior had been given the false tooth so he could eat and chew on the right side of his mouth.

 A number of serious diseases, like beri-beri and scurvy, are the result of a lack of something in food or drink. In 1905 it was found that a lack of fresh milk caused the disease rickets – which resulted in bandy or crippled legs in children. The introduction of fresh milk to schools each day virtually wiped out the disease.

 Malaria is named after the Italian words *mala* and *aria* – bad air. In 1880 it was found to be caused by the female mosquito.

Washing is vital for a great deal of medical care and general health. Until fairly recently the use of baths was unusual. In a number of towns and villages in England people kept their coal in the bath. The Emperor Napoleon did not encourage washing – one of his letters to his wife, the Empress Josephine, told her: 'Home in three days. Don't wash.'

French surgeon Ambroise Parc, who died aged 80 in 1590, was the first to use ligatures to stop patients bleeding to death after amputations.

One of the biggest bugs found in people's insides by doctors is the tapeworm. Around four hundred years ago there seemed to be a competition among doctors from all parts of Europe to see who could find the largest, A doctor in Vienna produced a seven-metre one – then a doctor in Paris came up with a tapeworm 34.5 metres long and weighing a kilo! But they all seemed to be beaten by a tapeworm found in a peasant in St Petersburg, Russia – his was said to be 72 metres long! Among the famous people who had tapeworms were King Herod the Great and Philip II of Spain (the king who launched the Armada against England).

The common housefly may be the biggest threat to human health – it carries 30 different diseases which can be passed to humans.

Australian aborigines used moulds found under the shade of trees to treat wounds hundreds of years before antibiotics were discovered in the West.

A Roman doctor's medical kit was dug up in Colchester in the summer of 1997. It was discovered that most of the instruments used had changed little, if at all, in 2,000 years!

In order to convince women that it was safe to be operated on using chloroform as an anaesthetic, Queen Victoria allowed Dr John Snow to give her chloroform during the birth of her son Prince Leopold in 1853. The Queen's action convinced people that chloroform was safe.

Prince Rupert, one of the commanders of the Cavaliers during the English civil war, had a disc of bone removed from his skull, a process called trepanning, twice in 1667. He lived another 15 years.

When Florence Nightingale first went into nursing, she found that 60 patients were put into one room. The walls of the 'hospital' were covered with slime or fungi; the windows were shut for months to keep in the heat. The floors were covered with bits of dried blood and all sorts of other rubbish. She also found that patients' mattresses were never changed and people were often put straight into a bed without the sheets being changed.

Early surgeons usually had only one coat for their work. Often it was an outdoor coat and was cleaned at most twice a year!

 During the 19th century, people who suffered from tuberculosis, a lung disease, were told to use cabbage leaves to cure the poor quality of their skin when they had the disease.

Dr Ludwig Guttman, at the British Government hospital at Stoke Mandeville, began work in 1943 to help those with spine or other severe injuries. To help his patients regain the use of their backs and limbs after surgery Dr Guttman taught them to throw medicine balls (a heavy ball used for physical training). In 1948 he organized games for all those injured, calling them the Paralympics.

 Using stitches to sew skin back together again was used as early as the 6th century by an Indian surgeon, using natural fibres. He also introduced the first plastic surgery.

 On average over half the people in Paris hospitals in the 17th and 18th centuries died of infection caused in the hospital.

During Victorian times, it was believed that letting mice run up and down people's spines and ribs could help people with bad backs!

 The world's first blood transfusion in a human took place in July 1667 when lamb's blood was given to a 15-year-old boy who had continual fevers. The boy survived, after having a burning pain for a while.

 For surgery, there are four blood types in humans that may be used for transfusion – O, A, B and AB. About four out of ten Britons have A and can receive either A or O blood. Those with AB blood can receive blood from anyone, though there are only about five in every 100 people who have this type.

During the Middle Ages, western surgeons tried the first transplants of living tissues. The unfortunate 'volunteers' were either slaves or servants.

 The first person to use a spray to clear surgeries of germs was the British doctor Joseph Lister. He went on to use antiseptic in his operations and sterilized his instruments before operating. His ideas were widely copied. Not all things changed – up to the early 1900s, doctors still dressed in their outdoor clothes and used no gloves or face masks when working.

The cause of bad eyesight was a mystery for hundreds if not thousands of years. Early in the 18th century it was decided to stop using some of the 'cures' which had been used by doctors. These had included putting hen's dung in the eyes, licking the eyes with the tongue, smoothing the infected eye with a gold ring, and recommending that the patient cure weak eyes by drinking a lot of beer in the morning!

Since 1926, all the money made from the book *Peter Pan* has been given to the Great Ormond Street Children's Hospital in London.

The first artificial hand was manufactured in 1505.

In 1504 the Barbers and Surgeons were amalgamated into one Guild in England. The link between barbers and surgeons is still remembered in some older barber's shops. The red and white pole used as a sign is symbolic of a bandage wrapped around an arm prior to bloodletting.

The world's first blood transfusion using human blood took place at Guy's Hospital, London, in 1818. It was, however, not until March 1917, at a hospital in Brussels, Belgium, that the first successful transfusion of blood from one human to another was achieved.

In May 1985, in Cape Town, South Africa, a man had surgery and was found to have 212 objects in his stomach – including 53 toothbrushes, two telescopic aerials, two razor heads with blades and 150 handles of disposable razors!

 During the hundred years from 1563 to 1663, many advances in medicine were made. They included:

1563. Ambrose Paré of France published five books on surgery.

1576. Cardano described typhus fever.

1584. Von Grafenburg of Germany introduced artificial respiration.

1595. Galileo, the Italian astronomer and inventor, invented a thermometer.

1598. De Baillou of France described the disease whooping cough.

1614. Santoirio of Italy discovered the importance of perspiration and sweating.

1616. Sir William Harvey in England discovered the way blood circulated in the body.

1629. The first spectacle makers were approved in England.

1642. Bontius first described the terrible disease cholera.

1653. Johan Schultes described surgical instruments and the methods used for surgery.

1659. Typhoid fever was first described by Jan
Swammerdam.

 The first recorded successful operation for appendicitis
was carried out by Claudius Aymand in 1736.

 King Richard II is believed to have died of
anorexia brought on by depression, aged 36.

 Nicholas Andry, a physician in Paris, invented the
word Orthopaedics in 1741 from the Ancient Greek
for *straight child*, for a method for the correction of
physical deformitles.

In 1799 Sir Humphrey Davy, the great English chemist
and inventor of the Davy safety lamp for miners which
saved thousands of lives, used the gas nitrous oxide
(laughing gas) as an anaesthetic for easing toothache.
The use of gas when teeth were being pulled out
was only introduced later. This was first done by two
American doctors, Colton and Wells, in 1844 when
they used a mixture of laughing gas and oxygen to put
a patient to sleep while they took out the teeth.

 Baron Larreu, Napoleon's surgeon, introduced
painless surgery to operations in 1812, when
he amputated the limbs of soldiers during the
retreat from Moscow by first freezing them.

The British scientist and astronomer Dr Herschel came up with the idea of contact lenses in 1827. They were not made until 1887.

 Many of the basic tools or methods used in medicine seem to have been around for ages. But most were only introduced 150 years ago. A list of basics would include:

1. The safety pin. Invented by American William Hunt in 1849.
2. Plaster casts. Dutch Army surgeon Mathyssen first used bandages soaked in plaster in 1852.
3. The hypodermic syringe was invented by Alexander Wood in 1855.
4. The International Red Cross was formed by Henri Dunant of Switzerland in 1864.
5. Lord Lister of England used the first antiseptic in his surgery in 1867.
6. The first skin graft was undertaken by a man named Reverdon in 1869.
7. Microbes were first named by Sedillor in 1878.
8. Osteopathy, the fixing of bones, was first introduced by Andrew Still, an American, in 1874.
9. The first sterilized surgical instruments were used by Evon Berzmann in 1886.
10. Dr Halstead at the John Hopkins University in the USA was the first to use rubber gloves during surgery in 1890.

11. Aspirin was introduced by Herman Dresser in 1893.

12. Appendicitis was first discovered in 1886 by R. H. Fitz in the USA.

 Surgeons scrub their hands for seven minutes and wear sterile gloves so no microbes pass from their hands to the patient.

 The advances in medicine over the past hundred or so years have added years to people's lives in the west. In 1870 the average person was expected to live 40 years; by 1970 it was over 70 years.

In about 1600 the treatment for cholera was a drink of rhubarb juice – if you were rich – or rose hip syrup – if you were poor. Rose hip syrup is still available, having been used for children's illnesses through the ages. The best protection against the plague was thought to be onions, which were supposed to clear the air of germs in ten days. Overall, it was reckoned the ultimate cure was powdered unicorn's horn!

In 1577, a vicar in London announced in a sermon that the cause of the plague was sin, the cause of sin was the acting of plays, and therefore the cause of the plague was plays! As a result plays were banned in London and theatres closed when deadly diseases struck.

 Aspirin, first produced as a pill in 1896, is found naturally in the bark of certain trees.

 African witch doctors send no bill if a patient is going to die.

Ambulances were first put into service by Napoleon's surgeon during Napoleon's Italian campaign of 1796–97.

Braille, the method of reading used by the blind, was invented by Frenchman Louis Braille, the son of a carpenter, who lost the sight in one eye in an accident when he was three years old. He became totally blind three years later. He invented his system of reading after hearing that French soldiers used punch marks on paper to read messages at night without using a light.

The doctor to Frederick the Great of Prussia had a very odd task to undertake before the King went into battle. He had to cut open the King's veins and bleed him because the King believed it calmed his nerves.

For hundreds of years it was believed that the reigning monarch of England had the power to cure the disease scrofula. King Edward I is said to have cured 1,736 sick people simply by touching them, while King Charles II is said to have 'touched' over 100,000 sufferers. The last monarch to touch people was Queen Anne, who dealt with 100,000 people, including the writer Samuel Johnson, who remembered her as an 'old lady in a black cloak and diamonds'.

A German chemist, Dr Adolph Von Baeyer, who died in 1917, discovered barbituric acid, the basis for the group of drugs known as barbiturates. He named them after his wife Barbara.

 When it first appeared, Coca Cola, without the fizz, was sold as a medicine.

 The first patients to be fitted with artificial limbs by doctors lived in India over 3,500 years ago.

The first X-ray, by Wilhelm Roentgen, who had discovered these strange rays in 1895, was of his wife's left hand.

 Napoleon's private surgeon Baron Dominique Larreu could amputate a man's leg in 14 seconds!

 The ancient Egyptians used mouldy bread as an antibiotic to cure various diseases over 2,000 years ago.

 Chinese doctor Hua T'o, born in AD 140, was the first to use general anaesthetic while performing surgery. He used a mixture of the drug hemp and strong wine to put his patients to sleep.

 Russian doctor Zaharin, who died in Moscow in 1908, leaving a fortune of £200,000, was the most famous doctor in Russia. He was also one of the oddest. When he was asked to treat the Russian ruler Tsar Alexander III, he insisted that the conditions in the palace were the same as he had at home when he treated patients. So all the dogs in the palace were removed, all the clocks were stopped and all the doors were kept wide open. He left his overcoat, boots and hat in different rooms after he had taken them off and every few yards the doctor lay down to rest. He believed he should rest this way so that he would not feel tired later. When he was at work he told everyone that no one should speak to him unless he asked a question. They were to reply either 'yes' or 'no' and nothing more.

 In 1936 doctors in Australia were puzzled by Mrs Rebecca Parker of Sydney. She was extraordinarily buoyant in water. She was able to lie on the water of a swimming pool and rest her head on her arm without sinking. She then lay on her back and read a magazine. When she rolled over, she floated like a cork. The doctors concluded that she had an exceptionally low gravity but could not explain why.

The first ever living donor transplant was performed by Dr Murray and Dr John Merrill at Peter Bent Brigham Hospital in the USA. Richard Herrick was given a kidney by his twin brother Ronald.

 During the last illness of King Charles II, his treatment for the remaining five days of his life included having red hot irons put on his feet and the administering of 58 drugs.

A hospital diet in London in the 1660s included three pints of beer a day.

 Up to the mid-1770s, surgeons operated on a stage in public.

Magnificent Monarchs

Early in her reign, Queen Victoria employed a man called 'Her Majesty's Bug Destroyer'!

Queen Anne outlived all her 17 children. She died in 1714.

Richard Branson's great-uncle Major L. H. Branson was 'Conjuror to the King' for Edward VII.

During the French Revolution the mob broke into the royal tombs in Paris and meddled with the remains of the French kings and queens. The canon of the royal church managed to rescue the small petrified heart of King Louis XIV and presented it to an English family, the Harcourts. The Harcourts kept the heart in a special case at their home in England and showed it to interested visitors. One of the vistors was the Dean of Westminster Abbey. The Dean was very old and not all there. When shown the grisly relic, he held it, then, for some unexplained reason, licked it, then swallowed it! There was no way the heart could be recovered and it was certain the thing could not be digested. Very soon the Dean died and was buried in Westminster Abbey, presumably along with the heart of a French king.

Frederick II of Prussia, who lived in the 18th century, was a bit strange. He took off his uniform and high boots only once a year – when he went to see his wife on her birthday.

 After she gave up the Swedish throne in 1654, Queen Christina of Sweden dressed as a man.

During the reign of Henry VIII, the mummified body of the wife of Henry V, Catherine de Valois, who died on January 3 1437, was found when Westminster Abbey was being rebuilt. The body was put in an open box where it remained on show for 200 years until it was reburied in 1776.

 The brain of the Italian prince Lorenzo the Magnificent, still kept in Florence, is half a pound heavier than average.

The magnificent Taj Mahal in India was built by Shah Jahan as a tomb for his favourite wife Mumtaz-i-Mahal. It took 22 years to complete and cost £600,000 for the wages of the masons alone.

 The first king of the Sicilies, Italy (1751–1821), thought up an unusual present for his wife Queen Maria

148

Carolina – he ordered two pizza ovens for the royal palace of Capodimonte! 60 years later a pizza was made in the Italian national colours – red, green and white – for the Queen of Italy, and named in her honour: a Margherita.

 After a visit to see Queen Elizabeth II, jazz star Duke Ellington wrote 'The Queen's Suite'. Only one copy of the record was made and it is now kept at Buckingham Palace.

 Handkerchiefs are believed to have been invented by King Richard II of England. Handkerchiefs are square because, in the 18th century, Queen Marie Antoinette of France decided they should be.

The British royal family have always been given presents. One of the strangest must have been the lamb given to Princesses Elizabeth and Margaret (the Queen and her sister) in 1939. Nothing that strange about a lamb, you may think. But this one was a bit special – it had a very odd diet consisting of watermelon, cake and coffee!

 Tutankhamen's body was discovered in 1922, 3,274 years after his death, by the English archaeologist Howard Carter. It was one of the most magnificent discoveries ever.

The long and the short of British reigns:

Edmund II Ironside. 7 months, 7 days in 1016.

Edward V. 4 months in 1483.

Edward VIII. 10.5 months in 1936.

Queen Victoria. 63 years. She came to the throne in 1837.

George III. 60 years. He came to the throne in 1760.

Henry III. 56 years. He came to the throne in 1216.

Edward III. 50 years. He came to the throne in 1327.

Elizabeth II. 60 years +. She came to the throne in 1952.

Elizabeth I. 44 years. She came to the throne in 1558.

Henry VI. 39 years. He came to the throne in 1422.

 Henry I died after eating too many lamprey eels, on 1 December 1135.

 Alexander the Great, King of Macedonia, managed to conquer more territory than any other monarch – he was only beaten by Genghis Khan. He managed to take over about 2.2 million square miles.

King Constantine of Greece won a gold medal in yachting at the 1960 Olympics.

King Edward VII kept his clocks fast so he could be early to go shooting. He also kept a fireman's uniform waiting for him at Charing Cross fire station, so he could attend any important fires in London.

The King of Prussia, the father of Frederick the Great, wanted a private guard with men over 2 metres tall. In the attempt he made his guards marry women over 1 metre 80 cm tall.

 Charles II, King of England, Scotland and Ireland, made his French friend St Evremond the governor of Ducks' Island for a fee of £300 a year. The island was in the middle of St James's Park, London.

 George III bought over 67,000 books, including 200 Bibles. His collection can be seen in the British Library in London.

A 'communist' chess set made in 1960 in what was then East Germany had no kings. Workers took their places. The queens were kept as examples of well-educated and bright women!

 In Japan, only the imperial family are allowed to travel in a maroon car.

When the Queen is in the House of Lords, the Lords (or Peers) are not allowed to wear gloves.

In April 1988 the London High Court decided that the bones of St Edward the Martyr, the English king, should really be moved to a church. From 1930 until then they'd been kept in a cutlery box in a bank vault at the Midland Bank in Woking, Surrey!

Lady Jane Grey was Queen of England for only nine days. She was executed on 12 February 1554. Every queen named Jane has been executed, dethroned, imprisoned or murdered, or has gone mad.

The first English king to go through a coronation in England was Ecgferth of Mercia in 785. The chair of St Edward has been used for coronations in England for over 500 years.

 Among the places or areas named after kings and queens are:
1. *The Victoria Falls, Africa*. Named after Queen Victoria.
2. *Virginia*. The US state named after Queen Elizabeth I of England and Ireland (the Virgin Queen) by Sir Walter Raleigh.

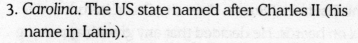

3. *Carolina*. The US state named after Charles II (his name in Latin).

4. *Maryland*. The US state named after Queen Henrietta Maria, the wife of King Charles II.

5. *Louisiana*. The US state named after King Louis XIV of France.

 Possibly the shortest reign was that of John I of France. He reigned, as a baby, for only five days before he died. He was said to have been murdered with a pin by his aunt.

 Charles V, the Holy Roman Emperor, born in 1500, was said to speak four languages. He ruled Spain, the Netherlands and Germany. He was said to speak German to his horse!

Queen Elizabeth I was the only British monarch whose nation did not possess land outside England and Wales.

Charles V of France, who reigned from 1364 to 1380, was not a healthy man. He had a disease which made the nails on his hands and feet dry up and fall out. In later life he always had an open wound on his arm. He died when he was only 43.

The first tsar of Russia, Peter the Great, introduced a tax on beards. He decided that any growth appearing within his kingdom should be shaved off with a blunt razor or the hairs plucked out one by one.

Queen Amelia of Portugal didn't like corsets, so she arranged to have X-rays taken of the ladies at court to find out who was wearing one.

Holland has now been ruled by women for over a century.

George II was once robbed in Kensington Gardens.

 Because George I couldn't speak English (only German), Great Britain's first prime minister, Sir Robert Walpole, spoke to him in Latin.

The famous story of King Robert the Bruce of Scotland and the spider was first told by Sir Walter Scott some 500 years after Bruce's death. It was claimed that, having seen a spider try and try again to throw a line of its web to a beam and eventually succeed, Bruce was inspired to fight the English one more time. He defeated the English army at the famous Battle of Bannockburn in 1314.

Eleanor of Castile, the Queen of Edward I, is said to have saved her husband's life during the crusade of 1270 by sucking the poison from a wound made by an arrow.

Mary, Queen of Scots, was known as the White Queen because she wore white when mourning the death of her French husband King Francis II in 1561.

The last British king to die in battle was Richard III, at the Battle of Bosworth on August 22 1485.

Charles VI of France had a problem speaking to his wife, Isabella of Bavaria. He could speak no German and she no French! In 1392 he went mad and killed four of his bodyguard when out in a forest.

When young, William the Conqueror was able to jump into the saddle of his horse while wearing full armour.

Charles I and Henrietta Maria did not meet until a month after their wedding! She was in France, he was in England! When they did meet in London, they couldn't miss each other – they both wore green suits.

The Emperor Napoleon of France designed the Italian flag.

James I had a tongue which was too large for his mouth. As a result he could not speak properly.

 In the 13th century Henry III of England had the biggest zoo in Europe. It included a lion and the first elephant seen in England which were given to him by Louis IX of France. He kept all his animals in the Tower of London.

 Isabella, the Queen of Castile and Leon, Spain, didn't spend much on sending Christopher Columbus on the voyage which led to the discovery of Haiti, the first part of America to be found by a westerner. The money was about the same as she spent on two dinner parties.

 The composer Mendelssohn taught Queen Victoria to sing.

Edward I of England was amazingly lucky. As a boy he was playing chess with one of his knights in a vaulted room when he suddenly left the table for no reason and walked away. Seconds later a huge stone fell right where he had been sitting! Another time he escaped being struck by lightning in Paris. It passed over his shoulder and killed two of his attendants.

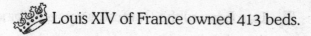

Louis XIV of France owned 413 beds.

Henry III of France liked to walk about the streets of Paris with a basket of puppies around his neck!

King Charles VIII of France had six toes on one foot. To help he wore square-ended shoes, which then became fashionable.

When Queen Eleanor, the wife of King Edward I of England, died, the King ordered crosses to be put up in her memory in the 12 places where her coffin rested on its journey to Westminster Abbey. The best known today is at Charing Cross station – it is a copy of the original, destroyed by Cromwell's soldiers.

Charles II had a small lab in Whitehall Palace where he experimented on human bones, eventually making a medicine called 'King Charles's Drops'.

King Louis XIV of France had a diamond-encrusted robe which cost one sixth of the price of the whole Palace of Versailles!

Attila, the King of the Huns, died on his wedding night, aged 47.

Richard III was born with teeth and hair.

King Edward the Confessor was an albino.

During the reign of Edward III of England, a law was passed making it illegal for anyone to eat more than two meals a day.

 After he died in AD 814, Emperor Charlemagne of Europe was embalmed. He remained as a mummy on his throne until 1215 when it was decided he should be buried. Even then his body was not left in peace. His coffin was later re-opened, his nails were cut and he was given a gold nose.

 In 1233 the Japanese royal family began to stain their teeth black, as a sign of beauty!

When he was young, King Henry VIII, a sportsman, was a champion hammer thrower.

Among his titles, the King of Siam was known as 'Possessor of Twenty-four Umbrellas'! His other titles were 'Brother of the Moon' and 'Half-Brother of the Sun'.

 Marie Antoinette, the doomed Queen of France, was very short-sighted but refused to wear glasses, preferring lenses to be fitted to the fans she carried.

The last independent ruler of Wales was Prince Llywelyn ap Gruffydd – he was killed in a rebellion in 1282.

 Henry VIII was the first British king to be called 'Your Majesty'.

King Alexander of Greece died of poisoning in 1920 after being bitten by his pet monkey.

 The wife of King Philip the Handsome of Spain was very attached to her husband. So much so that after he died in 1506, she kept his body in her bed for the next three years!

British kings and queens claimed the throne of France until 1801. *The Times* newspaper managed to print the royal coat of arms incorporating France every day until 1932!

 The 19th-century queen of Madagascar made it illegal for her subjects to dream about her.

Shah Jehan, the Mogul emperor, was buried in a tomb with one of his hands poking out, so people could touch or shake it. It became a bit manky after 40 years so was tucked back inside with the rest of him.

In May 1483 the boy King Edward V was locked up in the Tower of London. On June 16 he was joined by his brother Richard, the Duke of York. They never left the Tower and it is said they were murdered. Two skeletons were found in 1674 and they were examined again in 1933. They fitted what was known about the'princes in the Tower'. It is claimed that Richard III had them killed but there is no evidence that he issued such an order.

 The last Scottish king to be crowned on the Stone of Scone before it was taken south to England was John Balliol in 1292.

In 1797 Tsar Peter III of Russia was crowned. He had died 35 years before!

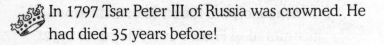 On average Queen Elizabeth of Russia (1709–62) changed clothes 12 times a day. She was the only person in Russia allowed to wear pink.

Queen Victoria became Empress of India in 1876. She then ruled over the largest empire ever known in history. All the bits of the world she ruled were coloured pink on maps. As it happened, less than a hundred years later George VI ruled over more countries in the world than she did.

 The Tudor kings and queens of England were descended from Ednyfed ap Cynwrig, Seneschal of Gwynedd, a Welsh royal.

 Though Henry VIII was very keen to have children, none of his children had children themselves.

 Just before her execution Marie Antoinette, the Queen of France, tripped over the foot of her executioner, then apologized.

King Henry II of England had a pet polar bear which he allowed to swim in the Thames at the end of a rope.

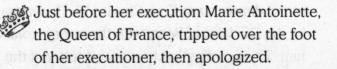 Elizabeth of York, the wife of King Henry VII of England, was the model for the queen on playing cards.

Louis XIV of France was the first person to wear high-heeled shoes. One pair had orange heels and wavy tops! He also wore tall wigs to make himself look more important. He and his wife, Maria Theresa of Spain, were the only people at court allowed to sit in chairs with arms.

Nicholas II, the Tsar of Russia, once thought of surrounding the whole of the country with an electric fence.

On January 28 1393, at a ball in Saint-Paul, Paris, the noble Louis of Orleans accidentally set fire to a group of men dressed up as 'wild men' in bits of cotton and feathers and performing a dance. One of the dancers was King Charles VI. He was saved by the Duchess of Berry who threw her cloak over him. The accident led to a riot which sent the King mad again.

 George V of the United Kingdom was a fanatical stamp collector. One day he remarked that some fool had paid an enormous amount of money for a stamp. He was reminded that that fool was himself!

King Haakon IV of Norway had unusual presents to give to friends – polar bears.

The ancient Egyptian monument Cleopatra's Needle, which can be seen at the Embankment, London, was around for 1,400 years before Queen Cleopatra was born!

Queen Victoria never allowed the royal train to go faster than 30 miles an hour. Once, when it reached 40 mph, she had the driver whipped and dismissed.

Fantastic Football

⚽ The first table football game, *The Two Man Footballer*, now over 100 years old, had only one side and one goal. Someone thought it might be more interesting if there were two teams and two goals!

⚽ Poole Town became the worst football team in British history in 1996. They were beaten in all their 34 games, scoring only 12 goals! 145 goals were scored against them. The team used 26 players, including 7 keepers.

⚽ Among the most unusual football teams was the 'Footballers' Battalion'. They started during the First World War, and played at Richmond, Surrey. A year after the war broke out, they were all packed off to France. These football players fought in battle together in France from December 1915.

⚽ The manager of the first professional football side in England, Blackburn Olympic, was John Hunter in 1882. He'd never played the game, but he had once been a member of a travelling circus!

During the Second World War, with so many players away in different parts of the world, football teams in Britain were short of players. To help play matches, they were allowed to use 'guest' players. This could go wrong: Charlton Athletic turned up to one game a player short. They saw a man waiting at the ground. He must be their 'guest' player, they thought. He was given a kit and went on to play. Only later was it found out he was the local milkman. He had only come to watch the game!

Sheffield Wednesday had a terrible game way back in 1892: they lost 10–0 to Port Vale. Their goalie had lost his glasses in the mud early in the game and couldn't see a thing without them! The score remains the biggest away win in the English League.

In a famous match, referee J. Thomson was 'sent off'. It happened in a game between Glasgow and Sheffield in 1930. Sheffield were playing in white shirts and black shorts; so was the referee. After the Sheffield captain kept passing to the referee, he asked for the game to be stopped. The referee was 'sent off' to put on a coloured jacket.

⚽ A million-to-one event happened twice to the same teams – Derby County and Charlton Athletic in 1946. During the FA Cup final, the ball burst. The game ended in a 4–1 win for Derby. Only five days later, in a League match between the two sides, the ball burst again!

⚽ The first all-seater stadium in British football was built by Aberdeen. 24,000 could fit in the ground, but it may have been a bit smelly – the ground was on a site with an old Celtic name Pittodrie – it means *hill of dung*!

⚽ Celtic are the only British football club to have no numbers on their shirts.

⚽ The Reverend Ashe of Langley did not like games on Sunday. On Sundays he would hide behind the trees at the football ground and when the ball came near, snatch it and put a pin in it! Teams soon began to take a spare to their matches. When the Reverend saw this he would say, 'Ah well, I suppose it must go on', and move off to his church.

⚽ Hull goalie Ian McKechnie had oranges thrown at him during the game because he liked them. He said, 'On a good day I get as many as 30 juicy Jaffas.'

⚽ During a game in December 1983, Mike Bagley of Bristol was booked for bad language. Annoyed, he grabbed the referee's notebook and ate it! His ploy failed – he was banned for six weeks.

⚽ Football dates:

1861. The first club football match took place, between Sheffield and Hallam, on February 12.

1872. The size of the football to be used in matches was agreed.

1874. Shinguards (shinpads) were introduced to football by Sam Widdowson of Nottingham Forest.

1878. Referees were allowed to use whistles at football matches.

1882. Crossbars were introduced to goalposts for FA Cup matches.

1886. March 27. First international football match in which all players were paid was held in Glasgow, when Scotland and England drew. Each player was paid 10 shillings (50p).

1890. The goal net was invented by a man from Liverpool – a Mr Brodie.

1891. Linesmen were introduced to football.

1891. Ireland introduced the penalty kick to football.

1921. Yellow jerseys were introduced for goalkeepers.

1927. The highest transfer fee in British football was £350.

1928. Arsenal became the first team in Britain to wear

shirts with numbers in a match against Swansea Town.

1937. A record 149,547 paying spectators watched the Scotland v England match at Hampden Park, Glasgow.

1939. Numbers for teams were introduced.

1948. Players were allowed to call for the ball or shout instructions to a teammate for the first time in Britain.

1950. A world record crowd of 200,000 watched the World Cup final in Rio de Janeiro, Brazil.

1951. The white ball was first introduced, instead of brown.

1953. Adi Dassler, the founder of the German company Adidas, introduced studs which could be taken off football boots.

1959. Peter Knight became the first substitute in English football in the Charity Shield match between Wolves and Nottingham Forest on August 15.

1962. Denis Law signed for Man United for a record £115,000.

1966. Substitutes were allowed in all matches in Britain, but only if a player was injured.

1966. Stanley Matthews became the first footballer to be knighted.

1979. Trevor Francis became the first £1m footballer in Britain.

1991. Premier League formed in Britain.

1992. David Platt transferred to Juventus for a record (for a British player) of about £8 million.

1994. The first 'sudden death' major football match took place at the Asian Games.

1995. Time-outs were used for the first time in football – at the Women's World Cup in Sweden.

1995. Georgina Christoforou became the first woman linesman in British football.

1995. A football match was played at the North Pole.

⚽ Albert Camus was a great French writer, who won the Nobel prize for literature. He was also goalie for the Oran football club in Algiers, the capital of Algeria.

 In Bedford in 1610, two men were arrested and later fined for watching football on a Sunday!

⚽ Jimmy McGrory of Celtic was the best scorer ever in British football. From his first appearance for the side, in 1923, he scored 410 goals in 408 games and remains the only player ever to average more than a goal per game.

⚽ Near the beginning of the last century, a man called Albert Craig had a strange power – he seemed able to control very large crowds. In

1908, by shouting a few words, he managed to stop a pitch invasion at Chelsea all on his own! Chelsea football club later sent him a personal letter of thanks.

 The only throw-in to score a goal happened way back in 1938, when Frank Bokas of Barnsley threw in, and the ball hit the fingertip of the goalie before going into the net.

What's the best save ever? Ex-goalie David Barry, aged 36, had no doubt about his – while out walking he saved a two-month-old baby, Susie Pang, as she fell four metres from the window of a burning house in New Milton, Hampshire, in August 1996!

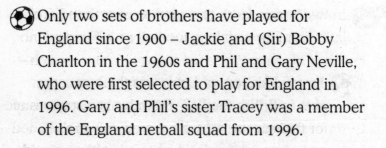 Only two sets of brothers have played for England since 1900 – Jackie and (Sir) Bobby Charlton in the 1960s and Phil and Gary Neville, who were first selected to play for England in 1996. Gary and Phil's sister Tracey was a member of the England netball squad from 1996.

 An FA Cup match in 1946, between Stockport County and Doncaster Rovers, lasted three hours and 23 minutes (203 minutes in all) instead of the usual 90 minutes. This was because the game continued at the end of extra time in the hope that someone would score since the teams were level on aggregate. In the end the match was stopped for bad light.

⚽ Terry Venables, who was to be England coach in Euro '96, was the first footballer to play for England in internationals from a boy to a full senior. He played his first seniors match for England against Belgium in 1964.

⚽ The first floodlit soccer match took place as long ago as 1878 with teams from several Sheffield clubs playing. Four lamps on 30-foot (nine-metre) high wooden towers shone light on to the pitch.

⚽ The most heroic football team ever was Start FC of the Ukraine. But they won no major tournament, no cup, nor did they appear in any well-known match – and only ever played against one side. During the Second World War they played only against teams of German soldiers and because they won were warned before one match that if they won again they would all be shot. They decided there was only one thing to do – win. At the final whistle they had won and before the Start team had left the pitch they were arrested. A short time later, still in their football strip, they were lined up and shot.

In February 1975 all 11 players and the two substitutes of Glencraig United, a Scottish team, were booked by the referee – not only before the game started, but before the team was on the pitch! They had been making fun of him.

One morning, with an away fixture to play, William 'Fatty' Foulke, a well-known goalkeeper, who appeared in three Cup finals, told his teammates he would not be joining them for an early morning training walk. When the rest of the team came back they found the giant goalkeeper asleep under the dining room table, having eaten all 11 breakfasts!

 John Goodchild was a keen Watford supporter in the 1920s. He was a most unusual supporter – at half-time he often tap-danced on the roof of the main stand.

El Salvador and Honduras, two countries in South America, went to war after a World Cup football match in 1969.

 Modern football is said to have started in Kingston upon Thames, where a Danish army was defeated in around AD 200. The Danish general was killed, his head cut off and kicked up and down the street.

In the 1966 World Cup final, Geoff Hurst scored three goals – one with a header, one with his left foot and one with his right foot. It was a record.

 The first TV coverage of the World Cup was from Switzerland in 1954.

Sir Frederick Wall, who ran English football for many years, did not like the idea of the World Cup. As a result, England did not play in the competition until 1950.

The first game of football in Brazil happened when a team of sailors from the British battleship *Crimea* played a demonstration game in front of the palace of Princess Isabella in 1878.

The great English footballer Sir Stanley Matthews was crowned 'King of Football' in Ghana in 1957.

The Second World War leader, Field Marshal Montgomery, was president of Portsmouth football club.

173

Instant replay was first used for football in 1965 by the US company CBS.

 Footballers in Britain threatened to go on strike in 1946 – they demanded a weekly wage of £7.20.

The England footballer Jimmy Greaves scored 44 goals for England, scoring in seven out of every ten matches.

Alan Shearer scored 30 goals for England by the end of his career.

 75,000 people watched the first FA Cup final at Wembley for free in 1923 by climbing over the walls. A single policeman on a horse cleared the pitch so the game could begin.

The first robot World Cup football competition was held in November 1996. Each team had three robots and three orange golf balls. The US beat South Korea in the final 20–0.

A football match was once played in Britain between one team that had no boots, with their arms tied to their sides, and another that had to play on two-metre-high stilts.

 A match between Cameroon and Guinea was held up in 1993 when millions of black butterflies invaded the pitch!

 The top wage for a British footballer in 1947 was £11.

 The first ever penalty shoot-out in England took place in 1972 in the game between Birmingham and Stoke.

 Women footballers were allowed to play on League grounds in Britain for the first time in 1971.

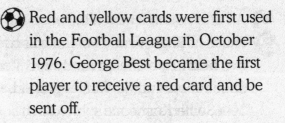 Red and yellow cards were first used in the Football League in October 1976. George Best became the first player to receive a red card and be sent off.

 Derby County, Preston North End and Aston Villa football clubs all started as baseball clubs!

⚽ Trouble at football matches is not new – in 1314 King Edward II of England banned football in London because of crowd trouble and rowdiness in the streets.

⚽ England women played their first match in the Women's World Cup in Sweden in 1995.

⚽ Liverpool spent £21,000 on players in 1947. In 1990 the club spent £9.5 million on players.

⚽ The famous Kop at Anfield was put up in 1906, in memory of local men who had died on the hill in the battle of Spioen Kop in the Boer war. It had no roof until 1928.

⚽ The USA won the first Women's World Cup in 1991. They beat Norway 2–1 in the final, held in China.

⚽ An international match between the Under-21 teams of England and Poland was held up for two hours by a cheese sandwich! The game was about to start at the Wolves ground, in October 1996, when someone spotted a strange metal package under one of the seats. The ground was cleared and the game stopped until the object could be looked at. It turned out to be a cheese sandwich wrapped in kitchen foil.

⚽ Almost all clubs have nicknames, like Arsenal ('Gunners'), Tottenham Hotspur ('Spurs') or Wolverhampton Wanderers ('Wolves'). Among the more unusual nicknames are:

Bolton – 'Trotters'

Brighton – 'Seagulls'

Dundee United – 'Terrors'

Sheffield United – 'Blades'

Stoke City – 'Potters'

St Mirren – 'Buddies'

Oldham – 'Letics'

Bristol Rovers – 'Pirates'

Rowdy Rugby

 Rugby League began in 1922 when the Northern Rugby Football Union was formed at the George Hotel in Huddersfield – 20 clubs voted to resign from the Rugby Union Association.

 The England rugby team were offered a £1m bonus in 1999 if they won the World Cup!

Rugby injuries are so common they rarely make the front page. But one injury did hit the headlines in April 1999 – Prince William had to have an operation after he fractured his hand playing rugby.

 George Henry 'Titer' West scored a record 53 points (10 goals and 11 tries) in a Rugby League match, playing for Hull Kingston Rovers in 1905.

 The New Zealand national Rugby Union side are known as the 'All Blacks'. The 'All Whites' are Swansea rugby players. (And the New Zealand Rugby League team are called the 'All Golds'.)

The name 'All Blacks' for the New Zealand rugby side was given to them by the *Daily Mail* newspaper on 12 October 1905 in honour of their victory the day before, when they had beaten Hartlepool clubs 63–0.

 Thomas Gisborne Gordon was probably the most unusual international ever. He had only one hand! His right hand was lost after a shooting accident when he was a child. He played on the wing for Ireland three times in 1877 and 1878. Ireland lost every match.

One of the great stars of world rugby was New Zealander Jonah Lomu. He claimed he was born to play rugby. Lomu's statistics are pretty impressive. His neck was 60 cm, his arms were 94 cm each, his chest was 135 cm and his hips were 125 cm! He has now retired.

 The Saracens rugby club launched a degree in rugby at Buckinghamshire Chilterns University in 1999!

The scores 4 and 7 were not possible in Rugby Union until 1971 when the scoring was changed. A score of 5 is now no longer possible.

There are six ways of scoring in rugby:

1. A try.
2. A goal.
3. A penalty goal.
4. A dropped goal.
5. A goal from a mark.
6. A penalty try.

Every South African side visiting Britain brings with them a mounted 'Springbok Head' which they award to the first team to beat them or the team which gives them the hardest match.

Australia have a phenomenal record when it comes to the Rugby League World Cup – they won it for 24 years in a row, before losing to New Zealand in 2008!

Tommy Holmes, a scrap merchant in the north of England, was known to accept any deal. His oddest purchase was a sick lion from a circus. Though he looked after the lion, the sickly creature soon died. Tommy arranged for the remains of the lion to be dealt with, but asked to keep part of its rump – which he took home and roasted. One of Tommy's other interests was Rugby League, and he headed a club in Workington. That Saturday, he went with the team for their match against Keighley. On the way he said he had a picnic for the team members. So they stopped and ate the food that Tommy provided – the lion sandwiches were quickly eaten!

 England lost a Rugby Union international for the first time at Twickenham in 1926. King George V was there to watch them lose to Scotland.

 The Leeds Rugby League club owns the Headingley Test cricket ground.

Willie John McBride scored his first try for Ireland when he played in his 62nd match for his country! It was in the Ireland vs. France match in March 1975. Ireland won 25–6.

Will Carling became the youngest ever national Rugby Union captain in 1988, when he became captain of England at 23.

Ninian Jamieson-Finlay played his first international Rugby Union match for Scotland against England when he was still at school – he was 17 years and 36 days old.

 The fastest try ever scored was by Leicester no. 8 Leo Price in the match between England and Wales in 1923. After a kick-off into a strong wind,

Leo chased the ball and attempted a drop goal. He missed, but ran on to catch the ball and score – all in under ten seconds.

The tallest man believed to have played in a rugby international was Richard Metcalfe who played for Scotland between 2000 and 2002. He was seven feet (2.13 metres) tall!

In November 1998 England beat the Netherlands by a cool 100–0 points!

Pierre Albadejo of France was the first player to kick three drop goals in one international, against Ireland at Paris in 1960.

Britain issued a stamp to celebrate the centenary of the Rugby Football Union.

Bob Hiller of England scored in every one of his 19 internationals. This included 32 points in succession. He scored a total of 138 of the 199 points England managed over the 19 matches! When he retired in 1972, there was a headline: *Hiller 138 points, rest of England 61.*

In 1972 the Wales Rugby Union side won its fifteenth match in a row in the Five Nations

Championships against France. They hadn't lost against France since 1908, a record-winning run for the championships.

 The first hat-trick of tries in the history of the Five Nations Championships was scored by Henry Taylor of England in 1881. It took a while for the second – scored by Chris Oti for England in the match against Ireland in 1988! It became known as the Six Nations in 2000 after Italy joined.

 Rugby is said to have come from a game played by Roman soldiers in Britain, called 'Harpastum'. During the 1300s women joined in the game.

Henry Vassall, the Oxford and England player, first thought up the idea of passing the ball in the early 1880s.

Two of the most famous of the Welsh fly halves, Carwyn James and Barry John, both came from the same village – Cefniethin.

Rugby Union dates:

1870   Rugby Union introduced to New Zealand by John Munro, who learned the game at Sherborne School, England.

1893   Referees were allowed to make their own decisions, without the help of umpires.

1897   Team numbers introduced to rugby when Queensland, Australia, played New Zealand at Brisbane.

1900   Rugby Union first played at the Olympics.

1909   The first ever game at Twickenham – between Richmond and Harlequins.

1921   Numbered shirts first used in an international – England vs. Wales at Cardiff.

 By all accounts the first people to play rugby in Fiji were the police.

 When rugby began, teams were of 20 a side, and there were three fullbacks allowed!

In 1932, the heads of Rugby Union in Britain banned the use of floodlights – yet the first rugby match played using floodlights had taken place as early as 1878!

In 1893, Billy Haus, who played for Penryn RFC, Cornwall, won a competition for the longest kick in British rugby – he managed 79 yards and 30 inches (73 metres).

The club motto of the Barbarians is: 'Rugby football is a game for gentlemen in all classes, but never for a bad sportsman in any class.'

There are 13 players in a Rugby League side and 15 in Rugby Union.

The Calcutta Cup trophy is awarded to the winner of the annual Scotland vs. England Rugby Union match. It is made from melted-down silver Indian rupees.

Rugby League dates:

1896   Rugby League Challenge Cup launched.

1906   Rugby League teams reduced from 15 to 13 a side.

1922   The name Rugby League football is adopted.

1964   Substitutes allowed in Rugby League.

1967   K. Jarrett, a Welsh Rugby Union player, signs to Barrow Rugby League side.

1968   Colin Dixon signs a record Rugby League transfer from Halifax to Salford for £15,000.

Direct kicking into touch was banned in Rugby Union in 1902.

 A record 104,053 spectators attended the Scotland vs. Wales Rugby Union match at Murrayfield on 1 March 1975. Scotland won 12–0. This is still the largest ever crowd to attend Murrayfield.

 The first England vs. Ireland international was played in 1875 at a cricket ground – the Oval, London.

The oval-shaped rugby ball, with its pig's bladder interior, was considered unusual enough to be shown at the International Exhibition in London in 1851.

 The first rugby matches had two umpires with sticks. They decided if a referee had made a right decision. The umpires then became touch judges and their sticks had flags attached to them.

 The ground is now known for athletics, but the first England rugby match against the All Blacks took place at Crystal Palace, London, in 1905.

 Guy's Hospital claims to have Britain's oldest Rugby Union club, being founded in 1843.

Early rugby matches at Rugby School could involve 300 players! There were no positions.

The All Blacks begin international or major matches with a 'haka' – a Maori war dance. The first line of the haka is: 'Ringa pakia waewae takahia!'

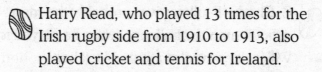 Harry Read, who played 13 times for the Irish rugby side from 1910 to 1913, also played cricket and tennis for Ireland.

 Rugby was first played regularly in Japan in 1924.

Rugby players Jack Gregory of England and Ken Jones of Ireland both won silver medals at the 1948 Olympics, as part of the 4 x 100 metre relay squad.

Red and yellow cards were introduced to the Rugby Union Courage League matches in Britain on 7 January 1995.

During the 1860s rugby teams could have 25 players.

The Australian Rugby League side is known as the Kangaroos.

 English rugby player Jason Leonard holds the English record for most caps – 114.

Wasps rugby club run their own fleet of taxis in and around London – decorated with the Wasps logo and black and yellow colours.

 Brian Bevan holds the record for Rugby League tries – a massive 796.

C. Charlie Faulkner was probably the most difficult man to challenge when he played for Wales. He was also a judo black belt!

 Teams of 15 a side for Rugby Union were introduced for the Oxford vs. Cambridge match in 1875.

In early 1995 Sheffield Hallam rugby players won their appeal for their game to be rescheduled – they were too drunk to play the first time!

 Junior Rugby Union player are known as colts.

The Soviet rugby team for the first women's world cup, held in Wales, were given free meals at restaurants because they were so short of money.

 In the 1990s, with the formation of the Super League for Rugby League and professional Rugby Union, the animal kingdom invaded the names of teams. The new names included:

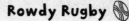

1.   Warrington Wolves
2.   Lancashire Lynx
3.   York Wasps
4.   Swinton Lions
5.   Keighley Cougars
6.   Batley Bulldogs
7.   Hunslet Hawks
8.   Northern Bulls

Others names included Salford Reds, Barrow Braves and Whitehaven Warriors.

Canadian Neil Jenkins scored a world record of 8 penalty goals in the 26–24 defeat of Wales at Cardiff on 10 November 1993.

Rugby is said to have started in 1823 when William Webb Ellis, a 17-year-old pupil at Rugby School, picked up the ball while playing football. He did so because he knew the game would soon end and he wanted his side to win. A plaque was put up to commemorate his achievement. Rugby was well known for the unusual – in 1797 a battalion of English soldiers with fixed bayonets were called to the school to put down a riot by pupils!

The England rugby captain of the 1980s, Bill Beaumont, was once described as 'John Wayne,

Goliath and Sampson rolled into one'. He was also said to have the biggest bottom in rugby!

 China became the 76th official rugby-playing nation in March 1997.

 Henry Garnett of Bradford was selected for Scotland in 1877. He played most of his international games in bare feet!

Among the oddest rugby supporters of all time was the Reverend Frederick Westcoot, the headmaster of Sherborne School in Somerset. He supported the team wearing a cycling outfit and a rat catcher's hat.

 Gerry Brand, the 1931–2 South African full-back, kicked the ball 90 yards to score at Twickenham. It is believed to be the longest ever dropped goal.

 Will Carling was England Rugby Union captain for a record 59 times. He was captain when England became the first team to win back-to-back grand slams in 1992.

 Princes William and Harry practised with the England Rugby Union side in 1995.

Rugby is reckoned to be the fourth most dangerous sport for neck injuries.

The Argentine touring team is known as the Pumas.

Playing against England in the 1932 Rugby League tour, Queensland forward Dan Dempsey broke his arm. Going off the pitch, he had it set. He then insisted on going back on the field. Tearing off the bandages and throwing away his splint he said, 'At least I can get in someone's way.' In the same match Australian Eric Weissel played with a broken ankle and the lock forward Frank O'Connor refused to remain on the stretcher as he was carried off the field.

One of the great stars of English rugby in the 1930s was Prince Alexander Obolensky. He had been born in Russia and never officially became English. He was killed at the age of only 24 in an air accident in March 1940 when flying for the RAF.

 An England Rugby Union side played South Africa during World War II. It was a little unusual – the match took place on board the ship the *New Amsterdam*.

 The nickname for the Twickenham Rugby Union ground is 'Billy Williams' cabbage patch'.

Crucial Cricket

 W. G. Grace played his first county match in 1864, aged 16.

 In a Test between England and India at Lord's cricket ground which ended on 31 July 1990, 1,603 runs were scored in 1,603 minutes!

 Cricket was first mentioned in 1598, in the borough records of Guildford, England. The game was known as 'creckett'.

 The first overseas cricket match was played in 1676, in Aleppo, Syria, when English merchants played a game.

 A Chinaman is the name given to a ball that breaks in a way opposite to that expected by the batsman.

 During a cricket match at Home Rule in New South Wales, Australia, a fielder came across a gold nugget worth £8. As a result the cricket pitch was closed and mining renewed.

 Ian and Greg Chappell of Australia became the first players on the same side in a Test to both score hundreds in each innings. Ian scored 145 and 121, his younger brother 247 not out and 133 against New Zealand in 1974.

 Dr M. E. Pavri, captain of the Parsee team, was pretty sure of himself. In 1889 he played on his own against a team at Metherau near Bombay, India. He scored 52 not out, and then bowled out his opponents for 38!

The largest-selling cricket magazine in the world is *The Cricketer*. It was first published in Britain in 1921.

Denis Compton, the great English sportsman, scored a record 18 centuries in the 1947 season, beating Jack Hobbs's 1925 record of 16. He also scored a record 3,816 runs altogether, beating a record which had stood since 1906.

 In 1884, all eleven players in the England Test side playing against Australia at the Oval had a bowl. Australia scored 551 runs.

At the end of July 1998 there was a cricket match at Wembley Stadium in London. It was a unique match, between the blind England team and a W. G. Grace XI of sighted cricketers. It was a warm-up for the England team before playing in the blind players' World Cup. The cricketers used a size three football for a ball.

Sir Arthur Conan Doyle, the author of the Sherlock Holmes stories, said in 1921 that the name Sherlock came from the name of a Middlesex bowler. This is unlikely, but the name could have come from parts of two other cricketers' names – Shacklock and Sherwin.

 Colin Croft, the West Indies bowler, managed to make the slowest score against Australia at Brisbane in 1979. He scored only two runs in 80 minutes.

 In 1899, Arthur Edward Jeune Collins, aged 14, became a schoolboy wonder, scoring 628 not out for his house at Clifton College.

 King Edward IV banned cricket in England in 1479, introducing a fine and up to two years in jail for anyone caught playing the game, then known as 'hands in and hands out'.

 It took until 1997 for England to win their first one-day international against New Zealand.

 The first international cricket match was between Canada and the United States in New York in 1844. Canada won by 23 runs.

In only his 18th Test match Garfield Sobers scored the then record of 305 not out against Pakistan at Kingston, Jamaica. The record was beaten by Brian Lara, with 375 at St John's, Antigua, against England. Sobers was the first to walk out to congratulate him.

 In July 1998 an archaeologist digging at Chelsea, London, came across what appeared to be a cricket bat – dating from 3540–3360 BC. It was made of oak and 75 cm long!

 The first recorded cricket match took place at Coxheath, Kent, in 1646.

 Lisa Nye, England women's wicket-keeper, set a world record of eight dismissals in an innings, against New Zealand at Plymouth, in 1992.

 The first cricket match at Lord's was Middlesex versus Essex on 31 May 1787.

 W. G. Grace scored the first and tenth of the first ten centuries scored by an English batsman.

 South Africa have been bowled out for less than 40 in at least four Test matches.

David Gower, the leading England batsman of the 1980s, loved having fun. In 1988 he had a bit of a problem. For a lark, after he had been out playing for England against Queensland, Australia, he went up in an ancient Tiger Moth plane. With him was fellow cricketer John Morris who had just scored a century for England. They buzzed over the ground where Lamb and Smith were still batting for England. The two surprised batsmen raised their bats and pretended to shoot down the plane! The two were recognized. It cost them a £1,000 fine – all for a £27 ride!

 Ian Botham was back in the England team in 1991 for the series against the West Indies. In the final Test at the Oval, London, he hit the winning boundary. It was the first time in 17 years that England hadn't lost to the West Indies. The match was also the last appearance of the legendary Viv Richards – he was retiring from West Indies Tests. His team had never lost a series while he was their captain.

The first twins to score a century for different sides in the same match were Mark and Steve Waugh of Australia. Mark scored for Essex and his brother scored for the Australian tourists, in 1989.

 The first ever county cricket match was between Kent and London in 1709.

The man who bought Lord's cricket ground in 1825 for £5,000, William Ward, was MP for the City of London. He sold the ground for £18,000 in 1866.

Micky Stewart, the England Test player and father of Alec, also played football for Charlton Athletic FC.

In 1893 W. G. Grace managed to score 93 – which meant he had then achieved every score between 0 and 100.

All seven Forster brothers played for Worcestershire. It is said their father, a vicar, tested their fielding and catching by using the family crockery.

A Surrey and All-England cricketer in the 19th century had the name Julius Caesar!

Doug Walters of Australia, playing the West Indies in the fifth Test at Sydney on 18 February 1969, became the first batsman to score a century and a double century in the same Test match.

The English film actor C. Aubrey Smith, nicknamed 'Round the Corner' Smith for his bowling style, looked after the British cricket team in Hollywood from the 1920s. His Hollywood home had a weathervane of three stumps and a cricket bat and ball.

The first non-white cricketer to play for South Africa in Tests was Omar Henry, aged 41, in 1992.

Ian Botham, the great England all-rounder, made front-page headlines in 1981, when he swung an almost impossible win for England against Australia at the Headingley Test. He blasted 149 not out in England's second innings. For the last three wickets England put on a massive 221. Australia still looked like winning – they only had to score 130. But they collapsed as England paceman Bob Willis took 8 wickets for 43 runs. England won this extraordinary and historic Test by 18 runs.

Charles Kortright of Essex bowled the only six byes in history, at Wallingford. His ball went straight over the batsman and the wicketkeeper. He was one of the fastest bowlers of all time.

 Cricket is about records and other numbers. These include:

61,237. The record total of runs scored by Jack Hobbs of England in his first-class career.

4,204. The most wickets taken in a first-class career – by Wilfred Rhodes.

643. The number of minutes Mike Atherton of England batted to save the second Test against South Africa in 1995 – he scored 185 runs.

501. The score which Brian Lara reached when batting for Warwickshire against Durham.

800. Muttiah Muralitharan of Sri Lanka's record for the most wickets in Test matches.

44. The number of wickets taken by Clarrie Grimmett for Australia in the Test series against South Africa in 1935–6.

20. The world record number of sixes in an innings – by Andrew Symonds of Gloucester against Glamorgan at Abergavenny in 1995. This record was matched in 2011 by Essex's Graham Napier against Surrey.

11. Jack Russell held this record number of catches in Tests, in the second Test against South Africa in 1995.

7. Dominic Cork of England took this number of wickets in the second innings of his debut Test, against the West Indies in 1995.

 On 26 February 1975, Ewan Chatfield, the New Zealand cricketer, 'died' on the pitch for three or four seconds, after being hit on the head with a ball. Given first aid, he recovered, with only a slight fracture of his skull.

 The poet Wordsworth was responsible for bringing about the Oxford vs. Cambridge cricket matches, in 1827.

The Oval cricket ground was originally a vegetable garden. Surrey played their first match there in 1846.

A game at the South Pole in 1969 had to end when the only ball was lost in the snow. The wicket was the Pole itself – a striped pole with a glass bowl on top.

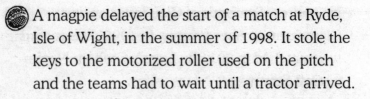A magpie delayed the start of a match at Ryde, Isle of Wight, in the summer of 1998. It stole the keys to the motorized roller used on the pitch and the teams had to wait until a tractor arrived.

One of the greatest throws in cricket was accomplished by R. Percival in 1884 – he threw the ball a massive 128 metres (140 yards).

Pat Morphy, a Kent cricketer, was able to hold six cricket balls in one hand. He is believed to have had the largest hands in the history of cricket.

In the 19th century the Oval cricket ground in London held walking races or poultry shows when cricket was not being played.

Early cricket bats of the 18th century were fairly large – over a metre tall.

Women are said to have invented overarm bowling in 1805, to avoid catching their fashionably wide crinoline skirts while playing cricket!

 Straight upright cricket bats, rather than curved ones, were introduced by John Small senior in 1773. They only came into regular use in the early 1800s.

In 1934 a cricket match in India was interrupted by five terrorists. Colonel Brett, who was batting, chased them off and was awarded the Empire Gallantry medal for his action.

 Frederick, Prince of Wales, son of George II, died in 1751 as a result of being hit by a cricket ball while playing on the lawn at Cliveden House, Buckinghamshire.

 During World War Two, the big roller from Lord's cricket ground was sent to the Far East. It was used to roll out the ground for airstrips for Allied planes!

William Adlam played cricket at the age of 104 at Taunton, Somerset, in 1888.

 The author J. M. Barrie founded his own cricket team, the Allah Kbarres – named after the Arabic for 'heaven help us'. His team included the famous authors P. G. Wodehouse and Arthur Conan Doyle. P. G. Wodehouse once scored 60 in a match between Authors and Publishers at Lord's, including one six and ten fours. He went on to take four wickets when bowling.

 Viv Richards, the great West Indies batsman, played football for his native Antigua in a world cup qualifier match.

The first googly was bowled in a match between Middlesex and Leicester at Lord's by Bernard James Tindal Bosanquet in July 1900. The Australians still call it a 'bosie' in his memory.

The first world cup cricket competition took place in 1995. The cup was a silver trophy found in a London jeweller's dating from 1882.

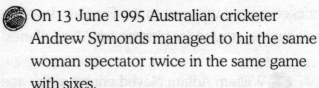 On 13 June 1995 Australian cricketer Andrew Symonds managed to hit the same woman spectator twice in the same game with sixes.

 By pure coincidence, the result of the 'centenary' Test of 1977, celebrating 100 years of England vs. Australia, was the same as the very first Test the two sides played – Australia won by 45 runs.

Don Bradman of Australia was both the youngest and the oldest player to score a double century, aged almost 22 in 1930 and aged 38 in 1946.

 Play at Lord's was first interrupted by a streaker in 1975.

 The first women's cricket match was held between two Surrey villages on 26 July 1945.

 George VI may be the only man to bowl out two kings – he dismissed his father George V and his brother Edward VIII in successive balls.

Charles Fry was an amazing British sportsman. In 1893 he equalled the world long-jump record, and in 1901 he played soccer for England and rugby for the Barbarians. He became England cricket captain in 1912, and scored the highest number of runs of any English player for six seasons!

 The world record price for a cricket bat stands at $145,000. It was paid in 2008 for the bat owned by Donald Bradman.

 While putting his sweater on, A. R. Gover managed to take a catch between his legs during a match at Kingston in 1946.

Ants stop play! Flying ants stopped a cricket match between Alvechurch & Hopwood and Dominies & Guild, at Worcester in August 1998.

 The father of the famous British author H. G. Wells was a professional cricketer.

 At a July 1995 match of 'Kwik Cricket' at the Oval with children, Wajid Khan, aged 10, bowled out Prince Charles first ball.

 In July 1981, Gladstone Small, the Warwickshire bowler, was fined £50 for wearing an advertisement on his bottom. The manager took sticky plaster and a pair of scissors on to the pitch to cover it up.

 On one of his school reports, a master wrote that Ian Botham would be 'nothing but a waster'.

 In 1990 David Gower was called in to play for England in a match at Barbados, West Indies, because so many of the England team were sick. He'd only been in Barbados to cover the England tour for the media!

 The batting helmet for cricket is said to have been invented by Mrs Hendren, wife of Elias 'Patsy' Hendron. She sewed on extra peaks to his cap to help protect his face while batting.

Cool Cars

 The first parking meters were installed in Oklahoma City, USA, in July 1935.

 The yellow wheel clamp, called the 'Denver Boot', was first used in London in 1982.

 A garage was once stolen, piece by piece. The Rolls-Royce which had been parked inside it was left completely untouched!

The world's smallest factory car ever made was the Peel Trident, a bubble car, produced in 1964.

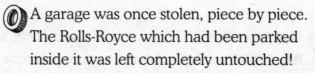 In April 1997, Mr Hope Till, aged 83, was given free road tax for life after buying a new Ford Fiesta. It was the 52nd Ford he had bought in a row. He had bought his first, a Ford Anglia, in 1950 for £365. Ford in Britain rate him their best private customer and in all he has owned 22 Escorts, 18 Fiestas, 2 E49A Anglias, 2 100Es and 8 105Es.

Metallic paint for cars came about by accident. One day in the 1920s a paint machine broke in a US factory. Bits of the metal were ground up and mixed in with the paint – it was found to be an attractive metallic finish for cars.

 One of the world's biggest traffic jams took place in January 1990 when thousands of East Germans filled their cars, all Trabants, with their belongings and headed away from the Communist East to the West. It was said that 'never had the little cars given so much joy'.

 Many works of art have used cars as a subject. Among them are Carhenge – a copy of Stonehenge made out of cars by American James Reinders in a field outside Alliance, Nebraska, in the USA.

 Sir Malcolm Campbell was famous in Britain and around the world in the 1920s and 1930s for breaking speed records in cars and in boats. One day he was stopped by the police and told off for going over the speed limit while riding a bike!

 In the 1940s ordinary detergent was added to oils in cars to help clean the engine and keep it clear.

 Many people have made funny insurance claims after their cars were damaged in accidents. One of the stranger claims must be that your car was run over by a tank . . . but it does happen! In 1995 in San Diego, California, a tank, stolen from the local National Guard armoury, careered through the city streets. It knocked down telephone and electricity poles, as well as flattening 30 cars before the police stopped the thief.

On December 22 1960 the Morris Minor became the first car to sell a million in Britain. To celebrate, the next 349 cars were specially made as Million Minis. They were a strange colour – lilac!

After a survey by the AA (Automobile Association) in Britain in 1968, it was found that the safest colour of car was bright orange!

Parking tickets were brought in to stop people blocking roads over fifty years ago. Among the stranger things to have been given a parking ticket are a horse (given a ticket in Hackney, London) and a train (Thomas the Tank engine, given one for blocking a road while being pulled to the Yorkshire Railway Museum).

When moving around off the track at Grand Prix races, former World Motor Racing champion Michael Schumacher rides a scooter.

In 1996 two Russian businessmen wanted their Jaguar XJ6 mended. Even though they lived in Siberia, in the Far East of Russia, they knew there was only one place to go. So they drove all the way to Yorkshire to get the car fixed at Les Thomson's garage. The distance was about 6,000 miles!

 A horseless carriage was designed by American Uriah Smith of Battle Creek, Michigan, in 1900. It had a model of a horse's head on the front so it would not scare the real horses!

The first British Prime Minister to use a gas-powered car was John Major. A gas-powered Rover 827 was delivered to 10 Downing Street in November 1996.

 Venice, the Italian city, has no motor cars – all trips are made either on foot, by horse and carriage or by gondola. Strangely the official name for a gondola carrying people is a gondola car.

 In 1901, a man named Emil Jellinek liked a new car he saw being made in Germany. He told the salesmen he would buy 36 of them on one condition – that the car was named after his daughter. The car company agreed to the odd request and named the car . . . the Mercedes!

On Christmas Eve in 1901, a young man staggered into the kitchen of his home in Detroit in the USA, clutching a small engine – which was dripping petrol on the floor – and a can of petrol. Putting it down, he asked his wife, who was stuffing a turkey, if she could hold the petrol can while he clamped the engine to the side of the kitchen sink and started it. She agreed. The 28-year-old man managed to start the engine and it ran for a full 55 seconds. He seemed delighted and enthusiastic about using the engine for his own motor car. His name . . . Henry Ford!

 An electric car was made in Austria as long ago as 1897.

 The Earl of Caithness invented a steam road carriage in Britain in 1860. It went at a top speed of 8 miles an hour and cost less than a penny a mile to run.

 The Aston Martin Lagonda, made in 1976 and costing £32,000, was said to be a 'super car', operated by computer. It was supposed to have a top speed of 140 miles an hour and be incredibly easy to drive. However, just before its opening test in front of the British press, the computer blew up and it managed to reach only one mile an hour – and that was when it was being pushed up a drive!

The world's longest car is owned by Jay Ohrberg of California. It's a 100-foot limo with 26 wheels and two drivers' compartments (one at each end, to help with reversing!). It also includes a jacuzzi, sun deck, helipad, swimming pool, king-sized bed and a satellite dish!

 Robbie Williams, the former Take That singer, can't drive. In 1996, he hired a £95,000 Ferrari 355 for show. In June 2011, he confessed to the *Sun* newspaper that he still can't drive.

 CAR DATES

1900. The first camera to trap speeding motorists was set up in Paris.

1904. January 12. Henry Ford set a new world land speed record of 92.37 miles per hour (mph) in his car the '999' on the frozen Lake St Clair in the USA.

1906. January 2. The French Darracq racing car set a new world land speed record of 108 mph, in France.

1907. The first speed humps to slow drivers down were introduced in the USA, in the state of Illinois.

1923. The first Highway was built in the USA – the Bronx River Parkway in New York.

1934. Driving tests were introduced to Britain after a rise in accidents.

1935. The 30 mph speed limit was introduced to British towns.

1936. Captain George Eyston set a new land speed record of 162.5 mph at Bonneville Flats, Utah, USA.

1937. The first speedometers were introduced to cars.

1938. Captain Eyston set a new land speed record in America of 345.4 mph in an eight-wheeled Thunderbolt car.

1967. The 70 mph speed limit was introduced in Britain.

1977. Stan Barrett, a Hollywood stuntman, set a land speed record of 638.637 mph, in a 48,000 hp rocket-engined three-wheeled car, at Bonneville Flats, Utah, US.

 The rickshaw was invented by an American Baptist minister in Japan in 1858.

 In Memphis, Tennessee, a law still existed in the 1980s which said that a woman was not allowed to drive a car unless a man with a red flag walked in front of it!

The first car radio was made in 1914. Student Alan Thomas of Toronto, Canada, fitted his Model T Ford with a radio receiver and overhead aerials. It only worked when the car stood still.

Craig Breedlove of the USA drove a three-wheel jet-powered car at an average speed of 526.28 mph on the Bonneville Salt Flats in Utah, America, in October 1964.

 Andy Coombes of Southampton made a motorized armchair in 1996! It had red velvet and braid, a drinks cabinet and a 49 cc engine for private roads and pedals for the public road. These motorchairs were for sale at between £3,500 and £5,000.

 British drivers have often captured the world land speed record. Some of the more famous records by British drivers have been:

1905. A. Macdonald, driving a Napier. 104.65 mph.

1924. Malcolm Campbell, driving a Sunbeam. 146.16 mph.

1926. Henry O.D. Segrave, driving a Sunbeam. 152.33 mph.

1931. Malcolm Campbell, driving a Napier-Campbell. 146.09 mph. Campbell was an exception driver – he also broke the world land speed record in 1927 and 1928, both times on the same day, February 4.

1935. Sir Malcolm Campbell, driving a Rolls-Royce Campbell. 301.3 mph.

1947. John Cobb, driving a Railton-Mobil. 394.2 mph.

1964. Donald Campbell, driving a Proteus-Bluebird.

403.1 mph. (Donald was the son of Sir Malcolm Campbell.)

1983. Richard Noble, driving Thrust 2. 633.46 mph.

 The first roadside petrol pump in the UK was installed in Newbury, Berks, in 1920.

 The first proper car radios were launched by the Philadelphia Storage Battery Company, Philco, in America in 1927.

 The idea that everyone in America who wanted a car might be able to have one was not thought of when cars were first made – for a start, they seemed too expensive. So it was not unusual that in 1889 *The Literary Digest* in the USA said the car was never going to be 'as common as the bicycle'.

 A number 8 in a number plate is considered lucky in Hong Kong and there is a big demand for any plate with this number. When the Hong Kong government sold the original number 8 plate in 1988, a businessman paid HK $5 million for it.

Three of the world's historic events which involved cars have been:

The assassination of John F. Kennedy

On a sunny day, November 22 1963, the American President was assassinated in Dallas, Texas, when riding in a motorcade in the centre of the city. Earlier in the day the President had decided against having the bulletproof roof on the car.

The Arrest of Nelson Mandela

While travelling by car from Durban to Johannesburg in South Africa on August 5 1962, Nelson Mandela, a leading voice of black South Africans and opponent of apartheid, was arrested by the police. He was later found guilty of treason and spent almost 30 years in jail before his release in 1989.

The Start of the First World War

Archduke Ferdinand of Austria, heir to the Emperor of Austria, was assassinated with his wife, in a car on the streets of Sarajevo, Bosnia, in 1914. Earlier in the day, another man had tried to kill the couple by throwing a bomb in their car. The Archduke caught it and threw it out. Oddly it was only because his chauffeur had taken a wrong turn that the Archduke and his wife came across the assassin. It was the murder of the Archduke which led to the First World War.

The use of private cars was banned in Germany in November 1939, a month after the Second World War broke out. During the war the Dutch royal family gave up using their cars – they travelled by bicycle or by horse-drawn carriages instead.

The registration of cars was begun in Britain in 1903.

A bicycle company called Starley and Sutton, at the Meteor works in Coventry, changed its name in 1885 to Rover. The first Rover car was made about fifteen years later and the first Land Rover was made in 1948.

The first car to be pressed out of steel sheets was made by Edward Budd in the USA.

The first woman Formula One driver was Lella Lombardi of Italy. She competed in Formula One races in the 1960s.

Up until 1926 cars which went over the mountain passes into St Moritz in Switzerland had to be hitched to horses and pulled along to the town with their motors switched off!

The Mini is the best selling foreign car in Japan.

A US motorist once took his car back to a garage in Virginia. He said the engine was making a funny whine. The mechanics opened the bonnet, looked around and found a kitten!

 The Newman-Haas Indy Car racing team was begun in the United States in 1983 by the actor Paul Newman and Carl Haas. Nigel Mansell, the British winner of the world motor racing championships, joined the team in a £3 million deal in 1992. Mansell went on to win the Indy Car championships at his first try.

 Cars were first started by ignition in 1949.

 Drivers and passengers in the front seats of cars in Britain had to wear seat belts by law from 31 January 1983. Rear passengers had to wear seat belts from July 1991.

 The type 41 Bugatti car has a white elephant on the radiator.

 During the Second World War over 649,000 jeeps were manufactured.

 Robert Neil, nicknamed 'Goldfinger', was jailed in Britain for seven years in 1992. He had organized a gang which smuggled

£35 million of gold into Britain hidden in car bumpers.

 The German company BMW began making cars in 1916.

 The man who is said to have invented the bikini in 1946, Frenchman Louis Reard, was a car engineer.

The first electric cars went on sale as long ago as 1899, being made by Walter C. Baker in America.

A woman from Yorkshire, England, passed her driving test in 1970 – after a record 39 attempts.

There are no roads in the City of London. Every road turns into a street when it reaches the City.

 In October 1997, Andy Green broke the land speed record in the British Thrust SCC jet car. The car reached 763 mph and was the first to break the sound barrier.

If you syphon the fuel out of one Jumbo 747 jet and put it into a Mini, you could drive four times round the world.

The first traffic lights were installed outside the Houses of Parliament in 1868. They blew up and killed a policeman – the signals had red and green *gas* lamps.

 The first amphibious car to cross the English Channel was the 'Amphicar' driven by two Frenchmen, M. Andal and M. Bruel, in 1962. It took them six hours to make the crossing.

 There were still 143 horse buses in London in 1913. In the whole of Britain there were over 100,000 motor cars.

 A French army captain, N. J. Cugnot, built the first ever mechanical road vehicle in France in 1709 – a tractor made to pull cannons. It went at four miles an hour. After Cugnot crashed it into a wall by accident, he was arrested and thrown in jail, becoming the world's first traffic offender!

 Between 1932 and 1934 there were no speed limits on British roads.

A spirit house is built at dangerous corners in Thailand, to ward off the evil spirits that cause traffic accidents.

The original 'petrol' engine was made by a man called Markus in Austria. It went on show at an exhibition in 1873. A lot of the car was made of wood. The fastest speed it could reach was about five miles an hour. Markus did not make any other cars, but his ideas were used by others to develop the modern car.

 Luc Costermans set a new world land speed record for a blind driver in 2008. He reached 192 miles an hour on a long, straight stretch of airstrip near Marseilles, France.

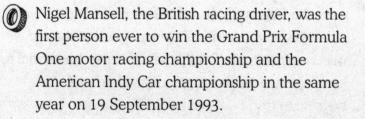 Ed Kienholz, an American artist who died in 1994, was buried in one of his old cars.

Nigel Mansell, the British racing driver, was the first person ever to win the Grand Prix Formula One motor racing championship and the American Indy Car championship in the same year on 19 September 1993.

 White and yellow car number plates were introduced in 1973. In 1967 it was found these colours were the most reflective.

 The first compulsory driving test carried out in the UK took place on March 15 1935. The first candidate was a Mr Bean.

The world's largest ambulance, the Jumbulance, can carry 44 patients and medical staff.

 The only person in Britain who can drive about in cars without number plates is the Queen.

 Henry Ford began the Ford Motor Company in the USA in 1906. His first car was called a Model N and sold for $600. Not many were sold. Three years later the company started making the Model T. Ford announced it was available 'in any colour, as long as it is black'. At first, the cars did not have hoods or roofs. They came later. The last Model T cars were made in 1927. A record 15,007,033 of them had been made. In 1925 a record 9,575 were made in one day. The top speed of the car was 40 mph. Oddly the car never had a dial to show how much petrol you had used.

Up to the 1960s, many cars still needed to be started by a crank if the day was cold or wet. The crank was put in the front of the car, below the radiator, and was turned to start the car up. Cars still had back back seats too – children could ride in small seats that were really part of the boot. These were often called rumble seats.

The first car number plates were seen in Paris in 1893; they first came to Britain ten years later. The first British number plate was A1. The car number plate A1 was sold for a world record £160,000 in 1989.

 The ancient school of the famous Greek philosopher Aristotle was found under a car park in early 1997.

The car is the safest place if there is a thunderstorm. During a thunderstorm the best place to park is away from trees.

Famous makes of toy cars:
1.   Dinky
2.   Corgi
3.   Matchbox
4.   Hot Wheels
5.   Tonka

Incredible Inventions

The steel nib pen was invented in 1803. Up to then the only practical writing instrument was a feather quill pen.

Jethro Tull invented the seed drill in 1701, allowing crops to be sown in rows without wasting seed.

Clarence Birdseye discovered the process for his frozen food in Labrador. He put fresh vegetables in a bucket of water and then let them freeze solid. It took him about ten years to produce machinery that could imitate nature. Once this was done he established his frozen food company. His idea attracted the attention of the food company Postum and he sold out for $22 million in 1929. The first packs of Birdseye frozen food went on sale in 10 grocers in Springfield, USA, on 6 March 1930.

In ninety years over twelve 'nose-picking' inventions have been filed in the USA.

There are many inventions where the inventor remains unknown. They include:

1. Spectacles.
2. The fork.
3. Glass windows.
4. Gunpowder.
5. The magnifying glass.
6. The glass mirror.
7. The wheel.
8. The bow and arrow.
9. Lemonade. It was invented in Paris in 1630, using sugar from the West Indies.
10. The cuckoo clock.

Nineteen-year-old Frenchman Blaise Pascal invented a machine to do sums in 1642 – it could add and subtract.

Christian Huygens of Holland invented the pendulum clock in 1656.

The American inventor of nylon, Wallace Carothers, was a shy and unsure man. He was working for the Du Pont chemical company when he discovered the chemical formula for nylon. The very first strand was squeezed out of a hypodermic needle in 1934. To start with, this first man-made fibre was used for toothbrushes and then stockings.

Carothers had no idea how important his work was and he became depressed. He felt a failure and killed himself in 1937. In 1940 alone 36 million pairs of nylon stockings were sold!

 It was German art publisher Rudolph Ackermann who first thought up the gears which, almost a hundred years later, were used for the first motor cars.

Levi and Strauss came up with jeans in 1850. Though first made with canvas, another cloth was needed for hard wear. This cloth originally came from Nimes, France, so they were called *de Nimes* or denims. They first went on sale to miners in San Francisco as 'bibless overalls'.

 Isaac Singer, the American inventor who perfected the sewing machine, had twenty-four children.

An American Mr Bean invented the first orange crate in 1875. Just as useful was the cheap cardboard box – invented by Scottish-born Robert Gair in 1879.

The cat flap was invented over 700 years ago! The famous scientist Sir Isaac Newton had one at his house in London in the 1700s. The modern cat flap may have been invented by the British film star James Mason, who made a spring cat flap for his Hollywood home.

Hungarian professor Erno Rubik came up with a mind-boggling puzzle, the Rubik Cube, in 1974. When it went on sale in the 1980s, over 100 million were sold.

George Eastman's Kodak camera went on sale in the USA in 1888 with the slogan 'You press the button, we do the rest'.

Three different people share the invention of television – the Americans Vladimir Zworykin and Philo Farnsworth and the Scot John Logie Baird. Neither Farnsworth nor Baird were quite given the praise they deserved. John Logie Baird originally began his experiments when poor health made him give up his business of making boot polish and jam! He was the pioneer of colour television in 1939. The work of Farnsworth was only recognized in the 1930s.

English carpenter John Harrison started early as an inventor. In 1713 he first went in for a government competition offering a £20,000 prize for the invention of an accurate chronometer, allowing sailors to know where they were. Two years later he produced his first invention, a clock with wooden wheels. After many years, in 1761, he came up with a remarkably accurate chronometer (to within one tenth of a second a day) and claimed the prize. It was only after he had appealed to the King, George III, that he was given the prize money.

 Henry W. Avery's first aluminium saucepan was made in 1890 – his wife was still using it in 1933.

 The historian to Louis XV of France became the first human to leave the Earth, on 15 October 1783, in a Montgolfier balloon. The five-minute flight took him to 24 metres.

Francis Carley of Australia invented a 'tail light' for sheep, to protect them from attacks by the wild dog, the dingo.

 That most useful of inventions, the safety pin, was invented in three hours by Walter Hunt in 1849. He had a $15 debt to pay off.

 Charles Darrow, an unemployed engineer, invented a game which he took to Parker Brothers in the USA. They named it Monopoly and it first went on sale in 1935.

The ejector seat was invented and developed by the British engineer James Martin, who died in 1981. The first tests of the seat were made with sandbags in May 1945. The first human used an ejector seat on 24 July 1946.

Los Angeles police once raided the home of the co-inventor of television Philo T. Farnsworth, believing his strange apparatus was an illegal still for making alcohol! Another co-inventor, Baird, had a different problem. Among his first inventions were inflatable soles for shoes – they burst.

William Moulton Marston, a US psychologist, invented the lie detector – the polygraph. He became better known for another creation – the cartoon Wonder Woman!

Sir Robert Watson-Watt devised the first effective radar system in 1935. The system helped win the Battle of Britain in 1940. His first experiments began when he was working on thunderstorms.

 When the Swiss introduced the world's first wristwatch in 1790, it was described as 'a watch to be fixed as a bracelet'.

A German chemist Fritz Klatte invented the world's first plastic – vinyl chloride – by accident.

Two concert musicians, Leopold Godowsky and Leopold Mannes, invented the first colour film for use in an ordinary camera, in 1935. They paid for their experiments from their concerts until they found a backer in New York. After nine years they went to work at Kodak. The people there made fun of them, calling them 'those crackpots' – until they succeeded.

The man who invented canned foods, Nicolas Appert of France, was a chef and confectioner. Despite being praised for his invention and given the title 'Benefactor to Humanity' he died in poverty in 1841. He was also the inventor of the *bouillon* cube (known as the Oxo cube in Britain).

The US Wagner Typewriting machine company came up with a new form of the machine in 1897. They offered it to the Remington company. After looking at it Remington decided the machine 'couldn't replace a reliable and honest clerk' and turned it down. Wagner was later sold to the Underwood company, who went on to sell 12 million of the new typewriters!

Italian physicist Alessandro Volta made the first electric battery in 1800.

The 'father of the computer' was Charles Babbage, an Englishman backed by the daughter of the poet Lord Byron, Lady Augusta Lovelace. He was unable to complete his 'analytical engine' after the government withdrew money from the project. An early version of the machine was used by Babbage and Lady Lovelace for an 'infallible' system for betting on horses. It lost them a fortune. Among his other inventions was the speedometer.

 Dr John Kellogg, the American inventor of cornflakes, was a bit mad, though, to his credit, he also invented peanut butter. At one time he claimed 'Nuts may save the (human) race.' He didn't say what kind of nut.

After the invention of barbed wire by the American Joseph F. Glidden in 1876, ranchers and farmers in Texas were not pleased to see the land dotted with it. One said, 'I wish the man who invented barbed wire had it all wound round him in a ball and the ball rolled into hell.'

 There was an invention for a mouse trap registered in the USA. Not so different, you might think, except this one used lassos to catch the mice!

For some time after the invention of the telephone people answered it by saying 'Ahoy'. It was the brilliant inventor Thomas Edison who suggested using 'Hello' instead.

 Fed up with the state of the British roads, in 1815 John L. McAdam devised a new road surface of interlocking stones. Tar McAdam (tarmac), named after him, came later.

 Machine guns, or rather machine bows, which fired 100–200 arrows a minute, were around in Ancient Greece and Rome.

 In 1910 a Mr O'Sullivan was annoyed by the vibration of the machines in the American factory where he worked. To solve the problem he brought in a rubber mat. But someone else had their eye on it and it disappeared. O'Sullivan could only find a small piece of rubber, so he cut it to fit the heels of his shoes – inventing the rubber sole.

Frenchman M. Monier threw his flowerpots about when angry. After breaking a number of them he found this expensive. He thought he'd try to make his own, using wire mesh and concrete. It worked – they didn't break, and he'd also invented ferro concrete.

This became the basic metal mesh and concrete mix used for bridges, skyscrapers and other buildings.

Inventions linked to the original inventor or manufacturer:

1. The mackintosh, produced by Charles Macintosh in 1823. No one knows where the extra K came from.
2. Morse Code. Invented by Samuel Morse of the USA.
3. The Hoover. Named after the man who first manufactured the upright electric vacuum cleaner.
4. The saxophone. Invented by Antoine Sax of Belgium in 1841.
5. The Bunsen burner. Named after the German chemist/inventor Robert Bunsen.
6. The Davy lamp. Invented by Sir Humphry Davy.
7. The Yale lock. Invented by Linus Yale in the USA in 1865.

George Stephenson built the world's first railway between Stockton and Darlington in 1825. The trains ran regularly.

When the great French film pioneer Georges Méliès was asked to sell his invention of cinema to one of the Lumière brothers, the old man refused. He told Lumière, 'Young man, you should thank me. This invention is not for sale, but if it were it would ruin you . . . It has no commercial future!' The Lumière brothers went on to give the world's first public showing of a film on 28 December 1898.

 Simon Ingersoll invented the pneumatic rock drill in the USA in 1871. It has not changed much in 150 years.

Nikola Tesla, who died in 1943, was one of the most important, but strangest inventors ever. Among his great inventions were the fluorescent light, the modern transformer, the modern power station, large elements of radio and aerial antennae. He spent almost all his life alone, seeing very few people. The only time he enjoyed appearing in public was when he gave weird demonstrations of electricity on stage.

Vicars and priests seem rather good at invention. Among them have been:
1. The Reverend William Fisken, inventor of the steam plough and central heating for churches.
2. The Reverend Edmund Cartwright, inventor of the power loom.
3. The Reverend William Lee, inventor of the frame for stockings; he made his first pair for Queen Elizabeth I in 1610.
4. The Reverend Timothy Bright, inventor of a form of shorthand.

5. The Reverend Stephen Hales, inventor of early air conditioning in 1761.
6. The Reverend Alexander Forsyth, inventor of the percussion lock for firearms.
7. English priest Roger Bacon, inventor of the early microscope and constructor of a flying machine.
8. The Reverend Berthou, inventor of collapsible boats.
9. The Reverend Stephen Hall, inventor of the blood pressure meter in 1761.
10. The Reverend Edward Booth, inventor of the repeating strike for clocks, about 1675.

 Kirkpatrick Macmillan, a Dumfries blacksmith, invented the first bicycle in 1809. The wheels were 32 inches in front and 42 inches at the rear. He had a carved horse's head on the front of the wooden frame.

For the man who invented so much to do with communications, Edison was a bit weird. He preferred to read in Braille rather than print and when he proposed to his first wife, he used Morse Code!

Printed and gummed stamps were the idea of June Longeville, the lady in waiting to Louis XVI. The world's first adhesive stamps went on sale on

1 May 1840 in Britain; they were printed by the US inventor Jacob Perkins. UK stamps are the only ones in the world without the name of the country of issue on them.

 German Karl Benz developed the first petrol-driven motorized vehicle, a tricycle, in 1878.

The explosive nitroglycerine was first made in Italy in 1847. The results were so horrifying to the inventor Sobrero that he forgot about it. Alfred Nobel rediscovered the process some twenty years later, developed a stable form, dynamite, and made his fortune.

Emil Berliner was the inventor of the gramophone, the first record player. He also had a great interest in health and helped introduce germ-free milk and dairy products in the USA. He always believed women were very good at science and gave a large part of his fortune to encourage girls and women to go into scientific research.

 A US customs man, Gail Borden, played an important part in the US Civil War of 1860–65. His invention of condensed milk and concentrated foods may well have helped the Union army win the war.

The inventor and businessman Alfred Nobel is remembered by the Nobel prize. His father also has a place in history – he invented plywood.

William Hoyng is now credited with inventing the modern surfboard. He thought it up while it was too windy to go into the sea on a California beach. The idea of using a wooden plank to ride the waves was very old – Captain Cook reported seeing Polynesians surfing in 1771.

James L. Plimpton invented the first four-wheel rollerskates in 1863 in the United States.

Perhaps because he was only 21, Italy turned down Marconi's invention of the wireless in 1895. He went to Britain, where, with the help of the Admiralty, he was able to develop his invention which was to make him world famous.

Benjamin Franklin, the great 18th-century American politician, thinker, scientist and publisher, was also an inventor. Among his inventions were bifocal spectacles, the rocking chair and the lightning rod.

The Dot and Dash in Morse Code recall the names of the two children of one of Samuel Morse's supporters – the 13th President of the United States, Millard Fillimore. Fillimore's children were called Dorothy and Dashiell. In turn, Edison named his son and daughter Dash and Dot.

While the bikini was worn in Roman times (there is a painting of a girl in a bikini in ancient Pompeii), it was 'reinvented' in 1946 by Frenchman Louis Réard. He named it after the Bikini Atoll, on which the Americans had just tested a nuclear bomb. The first public display of the bikini was on 5 July 1946, by model Micheline Bernardini at the Casino, Paris. The fabric design was based on newspaper print. The bikini became immediately popular, as did the model – she received 50,000 letters.

 The shoelace was invented in 1790. Laces were to replace buckles on shoes.

 Syvan Goldman, who owned a supermarket in Oklahoma city, invented the shopping trolley in 1937. The idea came from a pair of folding chairs he had in his office.

It's a beauty. Chester Carlson invented the Xerox photocopier in 1938. He developed the idea in the back room of his mother's beauty salon in New York. One of the first copies he made was of his application for a patent.

Alexander Graham Bell was not idle after inventing the telephone. Not only did he begin the *National Geographic* magazine, he continued to experiment with kites, electricity, speedboats and machines for much of his life. One of the stranger jobs he did was to design a special metal detector to look for the bullet that hit US President James Garfield in 1881. Unfortunately the bedsprings of the bed on which the dying President lay interfered with the machine, and the location of the bullet could not be determined.

The inventor of the biro, Hungarian Laszlo Biró, hypnotist and journalist, had no money and didn't seem to be that interested in his invention. The first biro was made in Argentina and went on sale in 1944 at $40. In 1947 he gave up interest in the biro and went off to become a painter.

Frenchman Louis de Corlieu invented flippers for use underwater in 1927.

Journalist Arthur Wynne invented the crossword puzzle in New York in 1914.

The modern hearing aid was invented by New Yorker Miller Hutchinson in 1901. The Queen of Edward VII, Alexandra, wore one during the Coronation of 1902 so she could hear what was going on.

American Charles Goodyear wanted to find rubber which would be useful in hot weather and at high temperature. One day, finishing work on his experiments, he dusted off some rubber and sulphur from his hands. It fell on to a hot stove. The rubber melted into a ball and reacted with the sulphur to create a new form of rubber. This vulcanized rubber was to solve his problem and be the solution to the making of millions of car tyres, among other products.

The inventor of yellow lines on roads was Bill Hadfield. He was paid only £2 for the idea by Greenwich council. Fifty years after he invented them he was caught on one. Bill did manage to make money, though; when he died aged 89, he left over half a million pounds in his will.

The Bath Oliver health biscuit was thought up by Dr William Oliver as he lay dying in his Mineral Water Hospital in Bath in the 1760s. To be sure it would be made, he dictated the recipe to his coachman before he died.

From the 1870s, students at Yale University in the USA used the empty pie tins from the Frisbie Pie Co. to throw to each other. It was not until 1948 that Fred Morrison took up the idea and produced what he called Morrison's Flyin' Saucer. The name was later changed to the Frisbee.

The French company L'Oréal introduced the first mass-produced shampoo in 1934; it was called Dop.

James I was the first English monarch to use a fork. The first picture of a fork appeared in the book *The Cooking Secrets of Pope Pius V* in 1570.

The aspirin tablet, invented by Karl Gerhardt in Germany in 1853, was first sold in 1915.

Percy Shaw, the inventor of catseyes on roads, died aged 86 in 1976. He first thought of the idea when at night, the lights from his car were reflected in a cat's eyes. He had a fortune and owned a Rolls-Royce, but had no curtains or carpets in his house. He had four TVs which he kept on a high volume all the time. He also insisted his factory was built round a sycamore tree he had climbed as a child.

 Fish fingers went on sale for the first time in Britain on 26 September 1955 in Southampton.

 Sir Clive Sinclair has a string of inventions to his name — the first commercial pocket calculator, the pocket and wristwatch TV, the first major home computer and the C5, a bicycle-like vehicle powered by a washing machine motor (which was a failure). His ZX81 home computer alone sold over 1 million.

 Although Galileo is credited with the invention of the telescope, it was first made by the Dutchman Hans Lippershey about two months before Galileo.

The elastic band was invented by London rubber manufacturer Stephen Perry in about 1845.

One of the first alarm clocks was invented by Leonardo da Vinci. It woke the sleeper by a soft rubbing of the soles of the feet.

Inventions sometimes come from watching nature. Sir Isambard Brunel, the British engineer, invented a machine for boring the first tunnel under the Thames after seeing the boring shellfish, the teredo, as a model.

A Sunday school teacher, Lemarcus Thompson, invented the rollercoaster.

Dastardly Deeds

 In January 1997 two Italians got away with £2 million of jewels from a Paris shop. They paid for the gems with a briefcase full of cash. But only the top notes were real – the rest were toy money!

Up to 1820 any person in Britain who owed over £20 could be put in prison for debt.

Until 1998 the death penalty still existed in the UK for those who had committed high treason or piracy with violence.

A British policeman went on trial in 1996 for stealing money from the police social club. He used the money to play a game on a fruit machine – it was called 'Cops 'n' Robbers'!

Paddington Bear was stolen from his showcase at Paddington station, London, in 1992.

One of the oldest prisons in the world is in Athens, Greece. Socrates, the Greek philosopher, was imprisoned there almost 2,500 years ago.

After his escape from a POW camp in the Boer War in 1899, Winston Churchill had a £25 reward, dead or alive, placed on his head.

Michael Mellor posed as a fake traffic policeman on a motorway in England for eight months in 1994. He would stop drivers and tell them off for their poor driving. He was eventually found out and fined £400.

Samuel Curtis was arrested in Philadelphia in 1924 for stealing a machine full of chewing gum. The judge sentenced him to eat all 250 pieces of chewing gum in the machine, which he had to pay for. After Mr Curtis had eaten them all, he was ordered to give the machine back to the owner. He was then freed.

Detective Eustace, who worked for the London police in Brixton, once caught a thief by posing as a statue.

When he stayed in the Lexington Hotel in Chicago from 1927 to 1932, the American gangster Al Capone had secret caves and staircases built. This work included a wall, behind which was a vault. Since Al Capone's fortune had never really been found, there was great excitement when the vault was going to be blasted open in 1986. The event was seen on live TV in at least ten countries. After the big bang, the vault was opened and . . . there was nothing there!

 St Nicholas (Santa Claus) is the patron saint of thieves.

 In 1911, three men were hanged for the murder of Sir Edmund Berry at Greenberry Hill, London. Their last names were Green, Berry and Hill.

 Among the stranger things to have been stolen are: a train in Florida; a bungalow, stolen brick by brick, in Bloxwich, West Midlands; and a fire engine, stolen while firemen were dealing with a fire in an old leather works in Hackney, north London!

James, Duke of Monmouth, and Lord Lovat were both beheaded for treason. Strangely, both had their heads sewn back on their bodies afterwards. The Duke of Monmouth's head was sewn back on so a picture of him could be painted. This picture is now in the National Portrait Gallery in London.

In 1933, a man in Paris tried to rob the house of an antiques dealer. The robber had a problem – his disguise was a suit of armour! The noise woke up the owner, who watched in amazement as the burglar climbed the stairs; then he knocked him down, put a small table over the fallen knight to pin him down and called the police. When the thief was asked why he had put on a suit of armour he replied he thought it would frighten the owner. The thief had another problem – part of his armour was so dented it took another day to get him out of it!

The Six Million Dollar Man, the American TV series, starred Lee Majors. It was about a bionic man with super powers. The series was filmed in California in the 1970s. In December 1976 an episode was being shot at an old amusement park funhouse. In one room stood a wax mummy. It had been there over fifty years. During the filming, it was knocked and one of the mummy's arms snapped and came off. The body of a real person was found underneath the wax! The mummy was taken to Los Angeles to be looked at. The body was of a man in his thirties. He seems to have been killed in a shoot-out in 1910 and then preserved and wrapped like a mummy to hide the crime. The body was buried in 1977. The crime remains unsolved.

A record 258 prisoners escaped from one prison in France during World War Two, as the Resistance, helped by British planes, blew open the jail.

The famous Spanish author of *Don Quixote*, Cervantes, was at times a criminal. In 1570 he killed a sheriff. His punishment was to have one of his hands cut off. He was later captured by pirates and became lame because of his ill treatment. He began writing his most famous book, *Don Quixote*, when in prison in Spain.

The Great Train Robbers were sentenced to 307 years in jail in 1964. In 1965, one of the robbers, Ronald Biggs, escaped with three other prisoners from Wandsworth prison, London. He had plastic surgery on his face and fled to Australia where he became a carpenter, and later to Brazil. In 2001 he returned voluntarily to England and was jailed. He was released in 2009 on compassionate grounds.

The crime organization the Mafia is said to be named after the saying in Italian 'Death to the French is Italy's cry'. The initials spell MAFIA.

Ernest Coveley of London robbed fourteen banks and building societies, using cucumbers! He wrapped two cucumbers in a plastic bag and waved them about like a sawn-off shotgun. This convinced the staff he was serious, and they gave money to him. After twelve robberies he ate his first 'gun' in a sandwich, then went out and bought some new cucumbers.

In 1790 the *Pandora* ship was sent from Portsmouth, England, to track down the mutineers from the now famous mutiny on the *Bounty*. The expedition easily found the fourteen mutineers who had stayed behind at Tahiti. These men were clapped in irons and locked below deck for four months. The *Pandora* continued the search for the other mutineers, sailing west towards Australia. The ship was wrecked on the edge of the Great Barrier Reef off Australia in August 1791. A few of the prisoners and some of the crew escaped, but were unable to survive in the hostile climate.

In Sweden in 1699, 300 children were accused of training cats to steal butter, cheese and bacon.

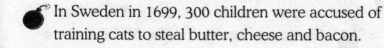 The last three 'witches' were put to death in England in 1682. Forty years later a woman became the last to be burned to death as a witch in Scotland.

When England were holding the World Cup football finals in 1966 the cup was put on show in London. It was stolen: the police found no clues and after two weeks still had no lead. Then, one night, David Corbett took his dog Pickles for a walk in Norwood, south London. David noticed a glint of something in the bushes, covered by a pile of newspapers. He walked on, but Pickles went to the pile of papers and sniffed and pawed. David called Pickles, but the dog stayed where he was. Mr Corbett went over and saw, at once, that the thing on the ground was the World Cup. He took it back to his flat and phoned the police. If it had not been for Pickles, the World Cup might not have been found. Pickles was given a major animal award, a rubber bone and £53 for food. Mr Corbett was later to receive rewards worth £6,000. Before the final, the West German team all met Pickles and touched him for good luck. Pickles had his moment of glory and was a real hero.

 Prisoners dug a 120 metre long tunnel to escape from a prison camp in Germany in World War Two. The escape was the biggest during the war.

The famous picture by Leonardo da Vinci, the Mona Lisa, was stolen from the Louvre art gallery in Paris in August 1911. The picture was missing for two years. It was found when the thief admitted he had the painting in Italy. He was given one year and fifteen days in prison.

In July 1976, thieves dug tunnels through the sewers in Nice, in the south of France. They got as far as one of the main banks, where they stole a record £6 million.

About a hundred years ago the Emperor of Ethiopia used an electric chair as a throne!

The *vendetta*, when one person kills another for revenge, may have begun on the island of Corsica. In the early 1900s seventeen people were killed in a vendetta on the island in an argument over who owned a chestnut tree!

Captain Thomas Blood, dressed as a priest, went to the Royal Treasure Room of the Tower of London in 1675. There was only one guard. Blood overpowered him, then stole the Crown jewels. Putting them in a sack, he tried to escape. He was caught before he left the Tower of London. King Charles II was so impressed by the daring deed of Captain Blood, that he said that Blood was not to be hanged for his crime. More than that, he gave this royal burglar a pension of £300 a year!

The American actress Zsa Zsa Gabor had a designer striped dress made in case she had to go to jail for slapping a policeman in Los Angeles. She was later sent to jail for three days.

 The first criminal on the run to be caught by the Internet was Leslie Rogg. He had escaped from a jail in the USA in 1985 and was on the run for eleven years. He was found in Guatemala in South America after his picture appeared on the Internet.

During World War Two British and other prisoners escaped from their jail at Sagan, Germany, by a tunnel. The tunnel was dug while the prisoners took exercise by jumping over a vaulting horse. The story of the escape was told in the book and film *The Wooden Horse*.

In 1873 a man named Joshua Coppersmith was arrested in New York for trying to raise money for a new invention, a telephone. An American paper said: 'Well-informed people know that it is impossible to transmit the human voice over wires . . . and that (if) it was possible to do so, the thing will be of no practical value.'

The most famous horse to be stolen was Shergar. The horse had won the Derby in 1981. He was stolen from a farm in County Kildare, Ireland, on 9 February 1983. No trace has ever been found of the horse. The owners refused to pay a ransom for the horse.

King Gustav III of Sweden thought coffee was a poison. He once sentenced a man 'to death' by drinking coffee every day. The man lived to be very old.

Only 15 prisoners survived the Changi jail in Singapore during World War Two. One of them was the writer James Clavell. He wrote the book *King Rat* about his life in the prison. Later he wrote the screenplays for films such as *The Great Escape*.

Seventy-five prisoners tried to escape from a prison in Mexico in 1975. They dug and dug until their tunnel was finished in April 1976. They must have made a wrong turn somewhere, because they came up in the court where many of them had been sent to jail in the first place! They were all returned to jail.

Fingerprinting was first used by an Argentine policeman in 1891. The first British person to go to jail because of his fingerprints was Harry Jackson. He had stolen six billiard balls from a house in London. His fingerprints were found, and afterwards he was found guilty. He was sentenced to six years in prison.

Frank Mullins escaped from Edinburgh prison in June 1945 through a 30 cm hole and down a 45 cm drainpipe. He had been on a diet for weeks and, before he left his cell, had put grease, meant for a skin complaint, all over his body.

The first toothbrush is said to have been made by William Addis while in the Newgate prison, London, in 1780. He made the toothbrush from bone and a few bristles of a scrubbing brush. After he was let out of jail he began selling his toothbrushes. Among the other things invented in jail was the tip of the billiard cue.

 A prisoner in a US jail in the 1940s was given solitary confinement for using the electric chair as a toaster.

💣 In the 1800s the town of Evanston, America, made it a crime to sell ice cream with soda on Sundays. The people who made the ice cream and soda did not want to be out of work. They thought of a way round the new law. They made the ice cream, then put syrup on top. They called it an ice cream sundae.

 In England in 1644 it was a crime to eat anything on Christmas Day!

💣 Butch Cassidy and the Sundance Kid, who stole over $200,000 from banks and trains across America, were supposed to have been shot dead by soldiers in Bolivia, South America, in 1909. In 1978 Butch's sister said he had not been killed, but had lived until 1937. She said two other bodies were buried in the place of Butch and the Sundance Kid.

 It was only by one vote that a group of Frenchmen decided that King Louis XVI should have his head cut off by the guillotine in 1793.

William Gillen, aged 26, was arrested by police in Glasgow for trying to rob a bank. The police put him into an identity parade. As no one from the bank could recognize him, he might have gone free, but he then called out from the line-up, 'Hey, don't you recognize me?'

A headmaster and teacher in India were arrested by the police in 1966. They had kept twenty-one students in chains for three days because they were not studying!

Super Spies

 Some of the earliest spies are in the Bible. Moses used twelve spies to go ahead of the Israelites on their way to the Promised Land.

 One of the best-known of the early English spies was King Alfred the Great. According to legend, he disguised himself as a harp-player and walked into his enemies' camps to pick up information.

 Names of the Secret Services:
CIA: Central Intelligence Agency (USA)
KGB: Soviet intelligence service (former USSR)
MI6: British secret intelligence service
OURA: The Italian secret service
FIA: The German secret service
Mossad: The Israeli secret service overseas
ASIS: Australian Secret Intelligence Services
ONI: The Office of Naval Intelligence (USA)
SDECE: The French secret service
SIFAR: The Italian counter-espionage service

 Daniel Defoe, the writer famous for *Robinson Crusoe*, who worked for a time as a butcher, became an English government secret agent.

He got on well enough to become friends with King William III, and also spied for Queen Anne and King George I.

 Sir Anthony Blunt, a well-known British art historian who looked after the Queen's pictures, was found in the 1960s to have spied for Russia for many years.

 An English spy, who became the Duchess of Portsmouth, is recorded to have earned a fortune for her information. In 1681 alone she received £138,668 – worth up to £100 million today!

 Sir Francis Walsingham, the master of spies in England for Elizabeth I, paid for the spies himself. It made him bankrupt and he died in poverty in 1590.

 The American CIA agent Martha Petersen used a piece of hollowed-out coal to pass messages to spies in Moscow.

 During the Cold War, East German agents used an infra-red beam to send messages from the East to West Germany.

 The weapons for secret agents can be tiny. The Soviets made a lipstick that held a real 4 mm gun!

During World War II, the famous underwater explorer Jacques Cousteau posed as an ordinary diver in the south of France – while working as a secret agent. His job was to monitor Nazi naval movements.

If a soldier in uniform is caught on a secret mission behind enemy lines he or she is usually treated as a prisoner of war. If the soldier is in civilian clothes, they can be tried as a spy and, often, face the death penalty. In 1776, American army officer Nathan Hale was sent on a secret mission behind British lines in the American War of Independence. He was dressed as a Dutch schoolmaster. After being betrayed by an American who recognized him, he was tried by a British court martial and found guilty of spying. Because he was in civilian clothes, he was hanged. He became a legend to the Americans.

 When Genghis Khan and his forces invaded Europe in the 13th century, he knew what to expect. He had recruited spies who posed as merchants and traders. The information reached him in under 24 hours by using a string of ponies. Normally such a journey would have taken ten days. Genghis Khan's arrangements were not forgotten. The idea of using a string of horses for quick delivery of messages was revived in the US Wild West hundreds of years later – as the Pony Express!

The famous English playwright Christopher Marlowe was said to have been murdered by three agents of Sir Francis Walsingham in a pub in Deptford, London, in 1593, after it was found that he was plotting against Queen Elizabeth I.

 After the Japanese attack on Pearl Harbor, American code-breakers cracked the Japanese Purple Code. This work was vital in helping the US forces defeat the Japanese in the Battle of Midway in May 1942, changing the course of the war.

 The British film star David Niven became an espionage agent during World War II. He spoke fluent German and is said to have taken part in raids behind enemy lines.

 World War II British agent Wing Commander Forest Yeo-Thomas was known as the 'White Rabbit'. An exceptionally brave individual, he worked for the Special Operations Executive (SOE) in France. He once escaped from the Germans by hiding in a coffin!

 Britain had no organized spy service from 1660 to 1914.

The real name of the famous World War I spy Mata Hari was Margaretha Geertruida Zelle. She was very stylish: she ordered a new suit and gloves to wear at her execution in 1917.

 During World War I, German secret agents caught in Britain were found to have used hankies covered in secret writing to receive their instructions.

Britain's modern intelligence service was established under Captain Vernon Kell on 23 August 1909. It was called MO5 before the name was changed to MI5.

The British spy Sidney Reilly, known as the 'Ace of Spies', worked as a docker, a roadmender and a cook on an expedition to the Amazon before he became a super-spy. He went back to Moscow in 1925. Nothing more was heard of him. Although his wife stated in a newspaper ad that he had been killed by Russian troops, this was not certain. In World War II it was said that Reilly had really been helping the Russians and in 1972 a Paris newspaper claimed that he had always been a Soviet agent. What happened to Reilly remains a mystery.

 Britain could make a real mess of spying. In the 1940s the man they put in charge of spying on the Russians, Kim Philby, was already a spy for the Russians!

John Dee, who was an astrologer and a secret agent for Queen Elizabeth I, signed himself 007 – 400 years before James Bond.

 Books can change history and can be deadly! In 1959 the American author Richard Condon wrote a spy novel, *The Manchurian Candidate*. Many still believe it to be the inspiration for the assassination of President Kennedy in 1963.

 The British writer Graham Greene worked as a spy during World War II.

 Among the rarest spy cameras were two made to look like Lucky Strike cigarette packets. They were made in the USA in 1949.

 A Victorian spy camera was only one inch (2.5 cm) across and was disguised as a lady's opera glass. It was sold for £23,100 in 1991.

 The British spy writer Bernard Newman, who was a relative of the famous Victorian novelist George Eliot, always kept his eyes open and ears listening. While on holiday in Germany in 1938 he made an amazing discovery. He came across some unusual concrete buildings surrounded by barbed wire. A hotel keeper was able to tell him that the place was used for testing big new rockets. Newman thought this was important and told the British secret service; they didn't think much of the story and did nothing about it. A few years later, the rockets – the V2s – began to devastate parts of London.

 One area where the Japanese secret service leads the world is very unusual – underwater surveillance!

 Over the years, spies have developed their own language. Some of the more unusual words used include:

Doctor – the police

Cobbler – a forger of false passports

Hospital – prison

Shoe – false passport

Soap – truth drug

Measles – a murder which looks like death from natural causes, such as illness or an accident

Lion-tamer – a muscle man used to 'soften up' enemies

British spies have their own club in London – it is called the Special Forces Club.

 There are two sorts of spying: basic intelligence, where the agent works for his or her own country; and counter-intelligence, where the agent tries to prevent the work of 'enemy' agents in all areas.

Great success as a spy can sometimes depend on very small things. During World War II, the British were fighting the Italians in the deserts of North Africa. One day a British agent, the son of the religious leader the Aga Khan, came across the shell of a bullet. When he looked at it he realized that it was marked with a letter that did not appear in the Italian alphabet, but did appear in the German alphabet. Italian guns could not fire German bullets. This evidence confirmed that the German leader Hitler had begun to send troops to North Africa.

 When a spy decides to go over to the enemy (or the other side), he or she is known as a defector. A lot of trouble is taken to make sure these people are safe and able to pass over their information. Almost all defectors are taken to 'safe houses' to tell their story. Later many defectors will be given new identities, places to live and jobs where no one suspects what they might have done in the past.

 During World War II, the British Scout Association was thought by some German leaders to be a spying organization.

Sir Richard Burton, the great Victorian explorer, worked as a spy. When in India, he was so good at his disguise as an Indian that often his commanding officer did not recognize him.

 Ten people who have been spied on by the CIA or FBI:

1. John Lennon, the Beatles singer
2. Frank Sinatra, the singer
3. The Duke of Windsor, former British king
4. Princess Diana
5. George Raft, American film star
6. Paul Newman, American film star
7. President J. F. Kennedy
8. Martin Luther King, civil rights campaigner
9. Bob Dylan, singer
10. Harry Belafonte, singer

 Cardinal Richelieu, the French politician who also appeared in the famous book *The Three Musketeers*, set up a big spy network in France. It was known as the *Cabinet Noir*.

False or untrue information is often sent out or publicized by agents to fool the other side. This stuff is called disinformation.

In the 18th century Antoine Rossignol in France decided how codes should work. He thought that it would never be possible to devise an unbreakable code. The best possible code, therefore, would be one which took so long to break that the information would be useless by the time the enemy had decoded it.

 Sir Noel Martin-Macfarlane came up with a plan to personally assassinate Hitler in 1938, with a shot from a flat he had in Berlin. The British secret service and Government rejected the plan.

 Ten famous real or alleged spies of the 20th century:
1. Cary Grant, movie star
2. Noel Coward, British writer
3. Walt Disney, movie maker
4. David Niven, movie star
5. Rex Harrison, movie star
6. Lucky Luciano, US crime boss
7. Robert Maxwell, tycoon and criminal
8. The Aga Khan, religious leader
9. The Duchess of Windsor, wife of former British king
10. Errol Flynn, movie star

The South Korean spy organization is known as KISS.

Sir Edward Stafford was the first known double agent in history. He spied for England and Spain in Tudor times.

 A spy can be a legend in his or her own lifetime. In spy language, a 'legend' is a faked life, or new identity. Spies have to get used to the details of being a completely different person.

For a short time during World War II, the head of the British Special Operations Executive, which looked after agents abroad and tasks like blowing up railways, was known as 'M'. Ian Fleming used the letter for the spy boss in the James Bond books.

 Sometimes stories can help in the real world. The US author Leon Uris wrote a story called *Topaz*. In the book he hinted that there were Soviet spies high up in France. The French decided to look. They caught spy Georges Paques. He was jailed for life for passing top NATO secrets to the Russians.

 A radio operator in a spy network is often known as a musician.

 In the late 1960s, the Russians and the Czechs had a plan to close down the London Underground and cut off London's water supply.

A place where secret messages are left is known as a drop. Some of them are fairly obvious – like holes in walls, or gaps in a flight of steps. Some drops can be marked with a secret chalk mark.

 Jules Silber, a German spy in World War I, worked in Britain as a censor of letters. One day a woman's letter caught his eye. She had written that her brother was working on secrets for the Navy. Silber went to see her. He pretended to be a British security officer. He told her what she did was wrong and that to avoid trouble she should tell him everything she knew about what her brother did. She did so. As a result Silber was able to pass on secrets about the Royal Navy's new 'Q' ships to the Germans. Silber was never found out. When he left his job as censor, all his office gave him a party. They never thought they were saying goodbye to a spy!

 Among the spies used by the Russians and Americans were caretakers and cleaners. Cleaners could often find important information in rubbish. In America, the traitor and spy for the Russians, Aldrich Ames, was caught by, among other things, a careful look at his rubbish bins.

Humint is human intelligence (information from people). Electronic intelligence, from bugs, spy planes, spy satellites, and so on, is known as Elint.

 A professional thief used by an intelligence agency is known as a cannon.

 People who plant bugs are known as 'plumbers'. The most famous plumbers in history are those who bugged the Watergate building in Washington. The Watergate Scandal led to the resignation of the American president Richard Nixon in 1974.

 Female spies are either Ladies or Sisters. The ladies have the jobs which need them to work quietly at home or abroad. The sisters have the far tougher job. They are field agents who are required, if ordered, to do almost anything. In Britain there are more female spies and espionage agents than male ones.

 The Russian spy Molody was also an inventor. His car burglar alarm won a gold medal at the Brussels International Trade Fair as 'the best British entry'!

The American spy headquarters, the Puzzle Palace at Fort Meade, did not exist for many years! It was supposed to be a big secret. But it was rather obvious. It was built underground and covered 12 acres. There were aerials and antennae all over the place. The underground tunnels were packed with computers. Around it was a three-metre-high fence, with barbed wire on top. Behind this was a five-strand electrified fence. Behind this was a third fence patrolled by armed guards with dogs!

 In 1960, in a brilliant operation, the Israeli secret service and commandos managed to kidnap the Nazi war criminal Adolf Eichmann in Argentina. He was put on trial and later executed by the Israelis.

 During the Korean war of the 1950s, the CIA found that their best intelligence came from children. So there!

Dreadful Disasters

✵ Not long before World War Two broke out, the British government allowed Germany to invade Czechoslovakia. The British prime minister, Neville Chamberlain, called the matter 'a quarrel in a faraway country of which we know nothing'.

✵ During the seventeenth century a fort was built on an island off the Scilly Isles. It had a series of cannons put on the battlements – but it was found that none of the cannons was able to shoot far enough to hit any ships out at sea!

✵ In 1993 the ninth commonest cause of injury at work in Britain was animals!

✵ Every now and then a famous person is said to be dead when they are very much alive. This happened to:

I. Lord Baden Powell
The founder of the Boy Scouts was said to have been shot as a spy during the First World War. The news was widely reported in the USA.

2. Daniel Boone
The famous frontiersman of US history was reported dead in 1818. Boone laughed when he read the report. He died two years later aged 86.

3. Wild Bill Hickock
A legend in his lifetime, this sheriff and marshall of the 'Wild West' read of his death in a paper in March 1872. He wrote to the editor to say he was very much alive.

4. Alfred Nobel
The inventor of dynamite and the founder of the Nobel prizes was reported dead by a French paper in 1888. His obituary sounded so bad that he founded the Nobel prizes as a result.

5. Mark Twain
After the family of this famous US author died in 1897, he went into retreat. A US newspaper then reported he had died penniless in London. Someone was sent to confirm the news. Twain replied: 'Reports of my death are greatly exaggerated.'

6. Bertrand Russell
This great English mathematician was reported dead in 1937. The report was reprinted when he actually died in 1970.

7. Robert Graves
The English poet and writer Robert Graves was reported dead during the First World War. He actually died when aged over 90.

8. Paul McCartney
The co-writer of many of the Beatles hits was reported dead by a US college magazine in the late 1960s. The rumour was believed in many places and the present Sir Paul McCartney was said to be an imposter.

9. Eddie Rickenbacker
Eddie Rickenbacker was a famous US air and motor racing ace. In 1942 his plane went missing and he was reported dead. The next month he and his companion were found to have survived on a raft in the Pacific for 23 days.

10. J.P. Narayan
Reports in 1979 that this leading Indian politician was dead reached the Prime Minister, who went to speak over his 'body'. Narayan soon recovered.

Beekeepers in Brazil were looking for a better type of bee in the 1950s. By 1957 they had a new type of bee which produced more honey. The only problem was that they were killers. Swarms of these bees killed a number of people in Brazil and then moved north as far as America where more people died from their stings.

 Some 700 years ago an English baron, Fitzwaine Fulk, died of suffocation in his armour when his horse got stuck in a bog.

 One of the strangest disasters took place at a factory in Boston, USA. The company made black treacle. An explosion emptied a 15-metre tank of the stuff. 20 people were killed and 40 injured after a 5-metre wave of treacle ran through part of the city. It swamped homes and buried a fire station.

 Some time ago in Leeds, a gang of thieves rented an empty shop next to a bank. They began to dig a tunnel below the shop into the bank. By the time they had completed the job the bank had closed for refurbishment and was empty of cash and other valuables.

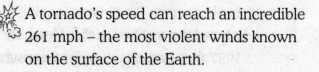 A tornado's speed can reach an incredible 261 mph – the most violent winds known on the surface of the Earth.

Maybe you can't be lucky all the time. £11 million UK lottery winner Karl Crompton managed to crash two new motorbikes, have one vandalized, spin a Porsche car, break a leg and dislocate a shoulder – all within a year of his win!

 The first man to be killed in a railway accident was MP William Huskisson. On 15 September 1830 he was at the opening of the Liverpool and Manchester railway and was wandering near the *Northumbria* train. Huskisson crossed the track to speak to the Duke of Wellington just as Stephenson's *Rocket* was coming down it. While others nearby got out of the way, Huskisson tripped and fell beneath the wheels of the oncoming train. Though taken by the *Northumbria* to an Eccles hospital he died later that day.

A Spanish air force jet once shot itself down after its gunfire glanced off a mountainside and came back and hit it.

The inventor of the top hat, James Heatherington, was arrested on 5 January 1797 for wearing his new invention in public in London. The hat attracted such a big crowd that several women fainted and a small boy had his arm broken in the crush. Mr Heatherington was told in court that his hat was likely to frighten people and he was fined what was then the huge sum of £50!

A record 324 twisters (or tornadoes) struck the USA in May 1957.

A woman in Romania was being carried to her funeral when she woke up, jumped out of the coffin and ran off along the road. Unfortunately she ran straight into the path of an oncoming car and was knocked down and killed!

Nine strange events as a result of hurricanes and tornadoes:

1. Clouds of tarantula spiders have been blown in by hurricanes in the USA.
2. In one hurricane in the USA birds sitting on a branch had all their feathers blown off!
3. In Iowa in 1962 a cow flew nearly a kilometre (half a mile) after being sucked up in a tornado.
4. A baby was once whisked up into a hurricane. He was found some way away, perfectly well, almost without a scratch.
5. After the Great Tempest in Britain in 1703 a cow was found alive after being blown into the top branches of a tree.

6. A British man slept through almost all the 1987 hurricane, until a tree crashed through his roof into his bedroom!

7. During Hurricane Inez in 1966, stranded people became so hungry that they opened cans of food with their teeth.

8. After a hurricane in Indianola in Texas in 1886 the town was abandoned.

9. A five-minute tornado in St Louis in the USA in late September 1927 killed 69 and injured 600!

The British Parliament looked at Edison's invention of the electric light. They believed it would have no use and would be of no interest to 'practical or scientific men'.

During the night of 15 October 1987 a great storm with hurricane winds hit Britain. It caused £1,000 million of damage, the highest figure ever recorded for weather damage in Britain's history. Before it hit, a woman rang the main weather forecast station and said she had heard there was a hurricane on the way. That evening, on the BBC TV weather news, the weatherman told the woman not to worry, there was no hurricane in sight! In Shoeburyness, Essex, the wind was the strongest recorded there for 500 years.

✳ An eccentric Englishman in the eighteenth century once set fire to his nightshirt to try and cure his hiccups. It is not known if he survived the cure.

✳ John Farynor was a royal baker in London during the time of Charles II. One night in 1666 he went to bed, forgetting to put out the fire in his bread ovens. At two in the morning, on Sunday 2 September 1666, the fire sent out sparks to a pile of hay in the building next door. The Great Fire of London had begun. House after house in the narrow London streets caught fire. The Mayor was told, but thought nothing of it, as such fires were quite common among the wooden houses. So it was not until that afternoon that the scale of the fire became obvious, as the warehouses along the river Thames caught fire. By Wednesday 13,000 houses had been burned, 57 churches were destroyed and shops were ruined. At St Paul's Cathedral the fire was so hot the ancient tombstones cracked and turned to dust, the metal decorations melted and the lead from the roof ran in rivers. The fire was only stopped from spreading by teams who knocked down buildings in its path. Though a disaster, the fire did have some good effects – the old slums of London were cleared and the plague was at last wiped out.

In 1912 the *Evening Sun* newspaper in the USA ran a headline: 'All saved from *Titanic* after collision'. It reported that the ship was still afloat and was being towed to a harbour in Canada. In fact, the *Titanic* disaster was one of the worst events to happen at sea; over 1,300 died. The *Daily Express* in England made the same mistake, saying that all the passengers had been saved.

In 1996 a group of clairvoyants (people who claim to be able to predict the future) turned up in Paris for a conference. They were a week late and had missed it!

A hairdresser, Leonard Moore, from Kentucky in the USA, decided to try and row across the Bering Straits from Russia to Finland in a bath. His only food seemed to be four gallons of peanut butter. The weather was so cold his peanut butter was frozen solid by the fifth day. The next day Mr Moore gave up his attempt when the water froze around his bath.

After the British set fire to the White House, the President's home in Washington, USA, in 1812, it was only saved from complete destruction because of a thunderstorm which put out the flames.

In 1970 the British Royal Navy began practice torpedo firing from a submarine off the Isle of Bute, Scotland. Something went wrong when a torpedo ran through the rough and stopped on the first green of the Kingarth links golf club where some golfers were just beginning their game! The Navy later turned up to collect their missing torpedo.

 When the first example of the duck-billed platypus arrived at the British Museum from Australia, the officials thought it was a fake and tried to pull its beak off.

 General Haig, a leader of the British Army in the First World War, did not think machine guns were any good. He refused to accept they would help in battle.

 President Johnson of America was once taken to see troops at a US base, being told they were on their way to Vietnam. In fact they had just come back. The President insisted on watching them take off again.

 Only one person has been killed by an earthquake in Britain – an apprentice killed in London by a falling stone during a quake in 1580.

When films were first shown, no one knew what effect they might have on those who saw them. Some people panicked when they first saw 'moving pictures', thinking the scene was real. A Dublin doctor took films very seriously. He said that people going to films should wear dark glasses and not watch the screen for more than a minute at a time in case they were blinded.

How to turn disaster into triumph. Lasse Viren of Finland tripped and fell during the final of the 10,000 metres at the 1972 Olympics. Though he lost about five seconds, he decided to get up and continue the race. By the next lap he had caught up with the main field and he went on to win in a world record time of 27 minutes and 38.4 seconds!

 One in five of all road accidents in Sweden is said to involve a moose.

Gold fever hit the area known as the Klondike in the Yukon in 1896. Charlie Anderson, a Swede, bought Claim 29 for $800 while drunk. When he had sobered up he tried to sell it but no one was interested, so he decided to have a go at digging there himself. In four years he found $1.2 million of gold in his mine. Alec McDonald of Nova Scotia did even better. He gave a hungry Russian prospector a sack of flour in exchange for Claim 30. He later walked away with an incredible $20 million. The chances of striking it lucky were slim – at most four people in a hundred in the Yukon actually found gold.

The great American writer Mark Twain decided against putting $5,000 into a new invention, the telephone, by Alexander Graham Bell. Instead he put $250,000 into another company which went bust.

When the first Impressionist paintings went on show in Paris in 1874 the critics made fun of the pictures and most of the public thought they were no good.

In the early nineteenth century an Irish professor, Dr Lardner, said that if trains went at a speed of over 130 miles an hour, the passengers would all be choked to death.

Some well-known people have died in strange ways. King Charles VIII of France was showing Queen Anne of Brittany on to a tennis court when he bashed his head on a beam and died soon afterwards from a fractured skull.

On 10 December 1903 a leading US paper, the *New York Times*, said that any research into 'aeroplanes' was a waste of time and money. Only a week later the Wright brothers made the first successful manned flight at Kitty Hawk, North Carolina!

The first hydrogen balloon was flown by Frenchman J. A. C. Charles over France in 1783. He climbed to 1,000 metres then came down in a field about 25 km from Paris. There the balloon was attacked by peasants who believed it was an evil spirit or a moon 'that had broken loose' and tore it to shreds. The King heard about the adventure and was so impressed that he introduced a law forbidding people to attack any air balloon.

The American inventor Lee De Forest was arrested in 1913 for trying to sell shares in a radio company. The court was told that his ideas were 'absurd'.

When the great composer Mozart died at the early age of 35 in 1791, his wife wanted him buried as cheaply as possible in Vienna. When the time came for his funeral it was raining, so she decided not to go. As a result his remains were put into a common grave for paupers. When she tried to find it later no one was able to say where he was buried.

✻ In the early 1800s a British scientist said that trying to light streets by gas was as impossible as using 'a slice of the moon' for light.

✻ Royal Ascot is one of the biggest horseracing events in Britain, held at the course at Ascot in Berkshire. In 1993 a woman tried to enter the Sovereign's Gate, to go into the Royal Enclosure. The woman was told by Eric Petheridge, 'I'm sorry, love, you can't come in here.' The person he tried to turn away was Princess Anne. He didn't recognize her.

✻ In 1920 the *New York Times* newspaper printed an article which made fun of the rocket experiments of Dr Goddard. On 17 July 1969, just as man was about to land on the Moon, the paper apologized for its mistake.

✻ Sometimes names are very important. For some reason certain names seem right, others not right. The following list shows how this can be true:
1. Robert Louis Stevenson's first name for *Treasure Island* was *The Sea Cook*.

2. Huddersfield rugby league club still play at a ground called Fartown.

3. The first name given to the great English racehorse Desert Orchid was Fred – thankfully someone decided to change it.

4. The Beatles song released under the title *Yesterday* was first called *Scrambled Eggs*.

5. Sherlock Holmes was originally called Sherringford, until author Arthur Conan Doyle changed it.

6. The name of a game invented by Major Walter Wingfield in Britain in 1839 was Sparistike. Someone decided it should have a better name – it is now lawn tennis.

7. When they first appeared, military tanks did not have a name. On being sent to France in World War One, they were delivered in crates which were said to contain water tanks. So they became known as tanks by accident.

8. Arsenal football club was first named Dial Square football club.

9. The band Rain changed its name to Oasis in 1993.

Berwick-upon-Tweed, the town on the borders of England and Scotland, is special. In official documents, the town is listed separately. So, in 1856, when the Crimean War broke out, Russia was at war with Great Britain, Ireland, the British

Dominions and . . . Berwick-upon-Tweed! When the peace treaty ending the war was signed later that year, the document missed off Berwick-upon-Tweed. Only in 1966 did Russia and Berwick-upon-Tweed declare peace.

 The Greek mathematician Pythagoras believed that some human souls became beans after death!

 When it was built, the great French palace of Versailles, near Paris, had no lavatories or bathrooms.

 In 1803 the French Emperor Napoleon sold the Louisiana Territory to the Americans for four cents an acre. It doubled the size of America and is thought to be the most worthwhile purchase of land in history.

 During the terrific earthquake in Lisbon in 1755, three quakes hit the city, followed by waves which reached up to 25 metres. Fires broke out in the city and many great works of art were consumed, along with thousands of rare and valuable books. The prison walls collapsed and hundreds of prisoners made their escape. After the earthquake there were 500 aftershocks, which were felt as far away as England and the West Indies.

Le Bateau (the boat), a painting by the great modern French painter Matisse, was shown upside down in the Museum of Modern Art, New York, for almost seven weeks.

The first rabbits, three pairs, were taken to Australia in the nineteenth century. In under ten years the rabbits had turned into an expensive plague – there were millions of them.

In Shakespeare's play *Julius Caesar* there is a line about a clock striking. Clocks did not appear until about a thousand years after Caesar's death.

In 1891 James Bartley was swallowed by a whale. He stayed inside the whale's stomach for two days. He survived and lived until 1926.

A woman who kept house for the Minister of War was sentenced to two years in jail and fined £500 for covering her pots of jam with bits of top-secret military documents.

Worcester cricket club found in 1889 that their pitch had been sown with turnip seed instead of grass seed by mistake.

Remarkable Rescues

(HELP!) In July 1998 milkman Phil George, on the Isle of Wight, put out a fire with twelve pints of milk and a crate of orange juice.

(HELP!) When the volcano at Nevado near Bogotá, Colombia, erupted in 1985, Bianca, the five-year-old niece of Alfonso Cardoso, was tied to a table to try to save her. She was found alive by rescuers 20 kilometres downstream from the mudflow.

(HELP!) In the Courrières mine disaster in France in 1906, over 1,000 miners were killed. When the surviving miners were rescued, they thought they'd been trapped for only four or five days – it had been three weeks!

(HELP!) One of the world's most famous monuments, the Eiffel Tower in Paris, was threatened with demolition in 1909. It was only saved because there was an important communications aerial at its top!

(HELP!) One of the items stored for rescue in the event of a nuclear attack in the United States was the recipe for Wrigley's chewing gum.

HELP! Fido, an eight-month-old rat, alerted a family in Torquay, Devon, to a fire in 1998. An electric heater had set fire to the carpet and furniture downstairs. Fido left his unfastened cage and climbed 15 stairs, each 20 centimetres high, to scratch on the bedroom door. The noise woke Lisa Gumbley, aged 29, and her daughters Megan, aged 9, and Shannon, aged 3. They were all able to escape. Firemen put out the blaze. Fido was given an Easter egg as a reward. The family dog, an Alsatian called Naseem, got nothing – he had failed to wake the family!

HELP! An American slave called Henry Brown rescued himself. He escaped from his master in the State of Virginia in 1858 by hiding in a box. The box was sent from Richmond, Virginia, north to Philadelphia. Henry had only a box of biscuits and a bladder of water to keep him going during his journey to the 'free world'. After his daring escape, he was known as 'Box' Brown.

HELP! One of the strangest rescues at sea happened in 1874. The clipper *Crusader* was on its way from Britain to New Zealand with 214 people on board. When the ship reached the stormy Bay of Biscay, off Portugal, it was swamped by the sea. The ship soon sprang a leak and was in real trouble when the pumps failed. Everyone was ready to abandon ship when, suddenly, the leak stopped. The water left in the ship was removed and the journey completed. When it reached the port of Chalmers, New Zealand, *Crusader* went into dry dock to be checked over. The hole was found, but all were amazed to find that it had been plugged by part of a huge fish!

(HELP!) Second Steward Poon Lim of the Merchant Navy survived for 133 days on a raft after his ship was torpedoed on 23 November 1942. Four and a half months later he was rescued off the coast of Brazil after drifting alone in the Atlantic.

(HELP!) In 1920, the 64-year-old president of France, Paul Deschanel, was rescued. He had fallen off the famous Orient Express train on the way to Lyons, France. He was found dressed in his pyjamas.

(HELP!) The Lutine Bell, at Lloyd's insurance of London, is rung whenever there is a disaster. There was an exception on 4 September 1996. The bell was rung to announce that Lloyd's itself had been rescued from financial disaster.

(HELP!) During the Second World War, a black dog called Jet found 125 people who were trapped under a pile of rubble when a block of flats in Chelsea, London, was destroyed by a flying bomb.

HELP! In one of the world's greatest rescues, 335,000 Allied soldiers and civilians were rescued at Dunkirk, on the north coast of France, on 4 June 1940, by a fleet of small boats and naval vessels.

HELP! During a wartime rescue, a handler and his dog were digging through rubble when a voice below them was heard swearing. An ambulance was called for the victim. When the pair finally reached their goal, they found it was a parrot!

HELP! The last man to leave the *Titanic* alive on that fateful night in April 1912 was Colonel Gracie of the US Army. He jumped from the top deck of the liner when she sank. Sucked down by the sinking vessel, he popped up again and miraculously found a cork and canvas raft. He then helped to rescue others from about 2.30 in the morning.

HELP! St Bernard dogs are thought to have been first used for mountain rescues about 850 years ago.

HELP! Barry, a St Bernard dog, became famous in the early 1800s for rescuing dozens of people buried by avalanches or injured in accidents in the Alps. When he died, his body was stuffed, and he is still preserved and on show in a museum in Switzerland.

(HELP!) In May 1916, after the wreck of his ship the *Endurance*, the British explorer Sir Ernest Shackleton and two others left the icy wastes of the Antarctic region to help rescue their companions. Those they left behind on Elephant Island survived on water and albatross meat. After weeks in an open boat, Shackleton and his men reached the whaling station at the island of South Georgia. A rescue party was sent and all the men left behind were saved. These men had survived for ten weeks sheltering under two upturned boats.

(HELP!) On 6 December 1941, during the Second World War, the British submarine HMS *Perseus* hit a mine off Greece. There were only four survivors. John Capes, a giant of a man, tried to help the three others, who were injured. With time running out, he drank a bottle of rum and went out of the escape hatch alone. He rose 50 metres from below and then began to swim. He swam for several hours, eventually reaching the Greek village of Skala. Capes was then hidden from the enemy by villagers. He later made it back to England, where he was greeted as a hero.

(HELP!) Two squirrels, named Fortnum and Mason, were saved by an RAF flight lieutenant in May 1940, during the dramatic rescue of hundreds of thousands of Allied soldiers from the beaches of Dunkirk. Mason was reported killed when a German bomb hit the boat he was on. Fortnum made it to Britain and was later taken on bombing raids over Germany.

(HELP!) *The Scarlet Pimpernel*, the story about the hero who rescued nobles from the guillotine during the French Revolution, was based on a real man. Baron de Batz, aged 32, managed to escape from the guillotine himself in January 1793 after trying to rescue the King of France, Louis XIV. Five months later he tried to rescue the Queen, Marie Antoinette, but failed. Due to his daring escapades, he was a wanted man. He was finally arrested in 1795. But he escaped (the only one of the nobles in the round-up to do so) and then lay low. When the monarchy returned to France in 1814 de Batz was knighted. He died at his estate, aged 61, in 1822.

(HELP!) After a wave of avalanches struck the Alps on 19 February 1999, a four-year-old boy was rescued from the snow in Vahur, Austria. He had been trapped for 100 minutes and was clinically dead. Revived, he survived and was taken to hospital. He had a miraculous escape, since people only usually survive for 15 minutes at most when buried by an avalanche.

(HELP!) The German chemist Christian Schönbein tried to rescue a bit of his kitchen in 1845. He was experimenting with nitric and sulphuric acid while his wife was out. She had told him not to play with any chemicals in the house. He spilled some of his concoction and, in a panic, used his wife's apron to mop it up. As the apron was now wet, he dried it before the fire. All of a sudden the apron burned up into nothing. He'd managed to discover 'guncotton', which went on to replace gunpowder!

(HELP!) During the summer of 1982 firemen rescued hundreds of pigs from a fire at a farm in Foston, Derbyshire, by making them breathe through the firemen's oxygen masks.

(HELP!) British sailor Tony Bullimore had a miraculous escape in the southern ocean off the coast of Australia in January 1997. Aged 57, he had survived five days trapped under his upturned yacht, the *Exide Challenger*. When he ran out of fresh water, he used a pump to desalinate seawater. The faint sound of the pump reached an Australian naval ship. Suddenly they realized that Tony was still alive. He had lashed himself into nets upside down to escape the sea.

(HELP!) When a new railway station was built at Knebworth, Hertfordshire, in 1978, it had to be built around the grapevines that grew at the old Victorian railway station. The station staff had made homemade wine from the grapes for years and wanted to save the vines.

(HELP!) In January 1998, Andrew Jepson, a 26-year-old construction worker, had an amazing escape. He accidentally slipped in front of a four-ton steamroller at a building site at Heathrow Airport, London. He thought there was no way he could survive as the machine, running at 6 kph, ran over him in just over a second! Luckily the uneven surface of the concrete and gravel below him acted as a cushion. Amazingly Jepson remained conscious. An air ambulance soon arrived. Paramedics operated on him there and then, and fluid was drained from his collapsed left lung. Six days later he was back at home. He said it was 'like being born again'.

(HELP!) Two German balloonists who landed in a Romanian swamp were rescued by the pilot of a British Airways plane which was flying overhead. He heard their SOS and alerted the airport at Bucharest.

(HELP!) At the height of the Second World War Dr Kingdon, born in Britain, set up a rescue committee in New York to save artists, writers and others trapped in occupied France. It was arranged to smuggle the people out of France over the Pyrenees mountains. Among the people rescued were the great painters Chagall and Fernand Leger and the writer Heinrich Mann.

(HELP!) In the 1300s big shoes were the fashion in France. They could be up to 60 cm long if you were a prince! At the Battle of Nicopolis of 1396, during the Crusades, the French had to cut off the ends of their shoes so they could run away! The army was saved by its smart thinking.

(HELP!) Hog-nosed snakes, found in America, save themselves if threatened. They roll over and pretend to be dead. If put back on their bellies, they give the game away, since they roll over and play dead again!

(HELP!) The International Rescue Corps was established for earthquake rescues in 1981.

(HELP!) During the Second World War a woman called Nerea de Clifford devoted herself to rescuing cats trapped in the rubble of bombed London.

(HELP!) In 1988, while firemen were out on a rescue, a fire burned down their fire station in Manchester, New Hampshire, USA.

(HELP!) To save them from destruction during the bombing of London in the Second World War, the Natural History Museum sent its collection of pickled snakes to safety in caves in Surrey. The artworks from the National Gallery, London, were sent to safety in mines in Wales.

(HELP!) A man sentenced to be hanged in Mississippi, USA, in 1894, was rescued after the hangman's noose unravelled and the man fell to the ground. He was then freed. Later, he was found to be innocent of the crime for which he had been condemned and was given $5,000 compensation!

(HELP!) A department of the Amsterdam Police in Holland is responsible for rescuing people who drive their cars into the many canals criss-crossing the city.

(HELP!) Mrs Murray may have been the unluckiest passenger of the 20th century. She was rescued from the *Titanic* in 1912, then rescued after the liner *Lusitania* was torpedoed by the Germans off the coast of Ireland in 1917, and then rescued from the ship *Celtic* when it collided with a steamer in 1927!

(HELP!) Richard Spruce, the British naturalist of Victorian times, saved many thousands of people through his work. He was able to send seeds of the South American plant quinine back to England. This plant was used to fight malaria, which is common in the tropics. The drug helped thousands of British soldiers. Spruce became a hero when he rescued the naturalist Alfred Russel Wallace, who had fallen very ill while on a trip to the Amazon.

(HELP!) During the Second World War hundreds of Allied soldiers, sailors and airmen were rescued from enemy-occupied Europe by an underground network of helpers who smuggled them along escape routes to safety. The organization was known as MI9.